AMERICA BEWITCHED

Also by Daniel Logan

YOUR EASTERN STAR
DO YOU HAVE E.S.P.?
THE RELUCTANT PROPHET

AMERICA BEWITCHED

The Rise of Black Magic and Spiritism

BY DANIEL LOGAN

William Morrow & Company, Inc.
New York 1974

BOOK DESIGN BY HELEN ROBERTS

PRINTED IN THE UNITED STATES OF AMERICA.

1 2 3 4 5 78 77 76 75 74

Library of Congress Cataloging in Publication Data

Logan, Daniel (date)
America bewitched.

Bibliography: p.
1. Occult sciences—United States. 2. Logan, Daniel, 1936- I. Title.
BF1434.U6L63 1974 133'.0973 73-12734
ISBN 0-688-00221-8

This book is dedicated with love to
Eileen, Roxanne and Karen Dent
Joni Evans
and
David Holumzer

PREFACE

IN THE LATTER PART OF 1971, THE AMERICAN PSYCHOANALYTICAL Association held a four-day meeting in New York City. Dr. Peter Hartocollis, a research director at the famous Menninger Clinic in Topeka, Kansas, addressed the group of almost two thousand psychoanalysts.

Dr. Hartocollis spoke of the current rising interest in areas of mysticism and the occult.

"The resurgence of mysticism in America," Dr. Hartocollis told his audience, "can be seen in the mind-expanding drugs, the proliferation of religious cults—such as the Jesus Freaks—and a growing fascination with astrology, Oriental philosophies, rustication, monasticism, and matters of the occult. It is mainly extant among the young, who are finding that material progress is valueless, science is immoral and the corporate organization of modern society is oppressive.

"In practicing love and peace, the mystics try to cancel the aggression of the world and to do away with their own. The mystical movements that are sprouting in the country represent an attempt by individuals to escape a world of aggression in order to renounce their own potential for violence."

Much of what Dr. Hartocollis said is valid and important. In my own work as a psychic and a parapsychologist, I have become aware of the need for young people to escape the materialism which is fast destroying the world in which they live. Love, brotherhood, and human compassion are disappearing as quickly as fresh air and pure water.

The search for spiritual enlightenment is not confined to the United States, it is a worldwide quest. Unlike the mystical fads of the nineteen-thirties, the present interest in spiritual and mystical awareness is of deep significance and lasting importance.

What surprises me about Dr. Hartocollis' report is his omission of an explanation of the differences in the various kinds of mystical experiences one can explore. He bunches together the materialistic psychedelic search (that is, through drugs), the religious quest (including the phenomenon of cults, such as the Jesus Freaks), and the inner psychic probings of the individual. It is most important to define these differences, and also to point out that when exploring the supernatural one can be harmed as much as enlightened. It is not only love and peace that attract mystics; there are those who seek to use mystical and occult teachings for evil purposes.

I well realize that science hardly, if at all, acknowledges the spiritual nature of man. I have spent half of my professional life as a psychic explaining or defending my psychic ability to scientific, intellectual, materialistic minds.

Usually, I hear such statements as "It can't be done!" "It's impossible!" "It's a trick!" Even after I have successfully demonstrated my psychic ability, I am invariably told that science has not yet proven the existence of the mystical or the supernatural, and there must be other explanations for what it is I do.

When I ask learned men to offer me another explanation, I am told that there isn't a material answer—*yet.* But there will be.

More than three quarters of the world's population believe in some aspect of the supernatural and strive toward a spiritual life of some kind. I do believe it is time that Western scientists paid more serious attention to such matters. They might better devote their time and energy not to scoffing or skepticism but to guiding and assisting those who are seeking out the negative aspects of the mystical experience at the expense of their physical and spiritual well-being.

The United States, like much of the rest of the world, may be facing a final crisis. The end of civilization, as we know it, has been predicted by psychics for countless generations. I have predicted it myself. The vast, unending spiritual or psychic energy, which lies for the most part untapped, can either help to save or destroy the world. If the new generation is not directed toward its highest spiritual potential, the next twenty-five years will be the last for the earth plane. This has always been one of my psychic impressions.

In Dennis Wheatley's brilliant anthology, *The Devil and All His Works,* he splendidly examines how the forces of good and evil have been utilized throughout history. He states that all forms of life depend on Light for their growth and well-being. When Darkness descends, all progress and growth are held in check. Decay and death occur in the winter, when the hours of Dark exceed those of Light. Since mankind's beginnings, Light has been associated with good and Darkness with evil.

The decision to write this book, which details my own experiences with Light and Darkness in the supernatural world in which I am professionally involved, was sparked by the many numbers of persons I have seen harmed by their misdirected or misguided investigations into the mystical. A person's life can be measured by the choices he makes. Confronted continuously with choices of every kind—physical, mental, and spiritual—he can take a step in the wrong direction of spiritual enlightenment and thereby prevent the progress of his soul, perhaps the only major sin that exists.

With the dawning of each new day, the Light does away with Darkness. It always has been thus and it always will be. Nothing is stronger than the Light. Even a modicum of light destroys darkness. My aim in this book is to help you to discover the difference between good and evil in any of your spiritual or occult endeavors. A basic knowledge of this difference will help you avoid mistakes that could cost you your soul.

AMERICA BEWITCHED

CHAPTER 1

"I'M THE DEVIL, I'M HERE TO DO THE DEVIL'S BUSINESS."

Within a half hour after those words were spoken by Tex Watson to Voityck Frykowski, five human beings, including Frykowski, lay dead—butchered, in one of the ugliest crimes of modern-day history. The murderers, besides Watson, were three extremely young girls, almost children—Susan Atkins, Linda Kasabian, and Patricia Krenwinkel.

The four youths had been sent to do the slaughter by their leader, their devil-Christ, Charles Manson. Manson had instructed one of the girls to "leave a sign, something witchy." The "witchy" sign turned out to be the crudely lettered, politically naïve word PIG, scrawled across the front door of the canyon house with a bath towel that had been dipped in the blood of actress Sharon Tate and her murdered, unborn baby. One of the "devils" committed a form of vampirism by licking the blood of her victims which had splattered over her hands and arms as she stabbed and slashed away.

The original plan of the murderers, to draw and quarter their prey after hanging them by their heels from the house beams, was not carried out, although Watson had on his person all the necessary equipment for such a deed. Nor did the killers gouge out the eyeballs of the dead and spread them over the walls, as they had often said they would when planning the event. Susan Atkins later expressed much disappointment over the lack of further mutilation. When the carnage of calculated murder—a total of one hundred and two stab wounds in a thirty-minute period—ended, the murderers left as silently as they had arrived.

I psychically feel that the reason the murderers did not commit all the horrors they had set out to do was because the "spell" or hypnotic state imposed upon them by Charles Manson was wearing off and they had to rush back to his side so that this evil psychic energy could be replenished. To reinforce his evil power over them, Manson sent his followers out a second time into the California hills on a succeeding night. That evening they murdered Mr. and Mrs. LaBianca; and if they had not been caught, no one knows how many more deaths would now be attributed to the foolish, lost souls who learned to harness the powers of Darkness. As it is, I am positive that they committed other murders that have not yet been traced to them.

Charles Manson was convinced that he was the Second Coming. His work with the evil powers of the universe led him to believe that the black race of the United States would rise up against the white population and eventually win out, taking over the government. The forces of Darkness informed him during drug-laden meditations that the blacks would then turn the reins of power over to him.

Charles Manson actually believed that he would someday rule the United States.

The Tate murders and those that were to follow would be blamed on the blacks, or so Manson thought. The whites would naturally retaliate and then the Great Revolution would begin, opening the door for Manson's rise to power. The dark, mystical messages that Charles Manson said he received while "tripping on acid" as he listened to Beatles records were all about the oncoming revolution and the need for him to be the new messiah.

It is most fascinating that he interpreted the words of the Beatles to have such dire meanings, for I have always regarded their music as spiritually uplifting, filled with understanding for not only the human body but the soul.

I am convinced that Charles Manson had harnessed the power of evil. That is how he was able to take possession of the minds of his followers and that is how he accomplished as much destruction as he did. This is not merely a psychic impression on my part, for Charles Manson's biography bears out his contract with evil.

From the age of thirteen, Charles Manson spent most of his time in reform schools and jails. He was a notorious car thief, pimp, and parole violator, and was incarcerated six years for his last crime against society. When Manson emerged from prison in 1967, he went directly to the hippie heaven of Haight-Ashbury in San Francisco. There he indulged himself in what he had studied while confined—black magic, witchcraft, scientology, hypnotism, astral projection, and many other aspects of the occult. He brought together his group of followers by using all of his newfound psychic powers. Six years of occult study had made him an expert in many of the teachings he now utilized in commanding his "family," as he ironically named this bunch of depraved, mentally ill monsters.

Evil does eventually destroy those who make use of its powers. By becoming the advocate and disciple of evil, Charles Manson condemned himself by the very power he sought to hold in his grasp. For it is in the nature of evil to allow itself to be used by those who would seek its strength, and then to destroy its advocates, proving its upper hand over all.

Like others who have used psychic power, Charles Manson had a choice. He chose to utilize the fantastically potent doctrines of occult teachings for his own advancement, at the expense of other souls, eventually his own.

Manson knew of karma and its teachings but misunderstood and misinterpreted its basic concepts. How else would he have been able to do as he did? *Karma* is the Indian concept of the totality of a man's actions in one of the successive states of his existence. It implies that he may learn from his mistakes, make right the evil that he has done, and reap the benefits of the efforts he has made by using acquired powers and opportunities. The first teaching of Karma is "Whatever thou shalt sow, thou shalt also reap . . . in this or another life."

"The karma is turning," Manson would say, relating it to the idea of the struggle between the whites and the blacks, the poor and the rich, the oppressed and the oppressors. Those now on the bottom (of whom he was one) would have their chance to rise to the top, and vice versa—instant karma, or so he thought. What he didn't take into consideration was that the process of karma may take many lifetimes, that justice is not always accomplished in the present life, and that the horrendous deeds he committed might force him, personally, to undergo many lifetimes to come.

Drugs destroy, rather than enhance, psychic awareness. They helped to kill any of the "good vibrations" which might have prevented Manson from continuing his ill-fated quest. Once one makes a pact with the powers of Darkness, it is almost impossible to retreat.

Charles Manson is a prime example of a metaphysician in reverse. Through hypnotism, black magic, and the base elements of the occult he was able to take over and control the minds of his group—just as Hitler grasped the psychic centers of hundreds of thousands of Germans. Manson's family, like the Germans of Hitler's time, were ready for a messiah, good or evil. The climate of "bad vibrations"—the lack of spirituality—was most evident in Hitler's Germany, as it is in many areas of southern California. But remember one thing—the Germans of the Third Reich still had the power of choice, as did Manson's family. But both groups *chose* to follow and worship their devil-leader. Many of those who originally congregated around Manson left when they realized the true evil that influenced the family.

When the spirituality of a people decreases, its opposite, materialism, emerges. The present lack of spirituality in many U. S. cities is a breeding ground for materialism. Worse, it allows the evil side of the supernatural to emerge.

Unfortunately, Manson's foray into the world of black arts is not just a case of one man gone berserk. So many are becoming immersed in gross materialism and its hopeless, decaying aftereffects that it is not surprising that its antidote—spirituality—is in the descendant.

Satan is not a person. The Devil is a psychic force. Lower California has a very high percentage of persons who desire to use satanic power. I have heard more stories about evil happenings which occurred in California than anywhere else in the United States.

Take the case of a world-renowned actress, for example. The story of an encounter with this brilliant, Academy-Award-winning star has been revealed to me by someone with whom I am artistically linked myself. My friend became directly involved with the actress—whose name I cannot now, for obvious reasons, divulge—in a nightmarish, frightening story. Someday, I fear, this actress will make international headlines because of her entanglement with the evil forces working through her.

Negotiations had been going on between the actress and my friend for some time; they were going to work on a project together. The actress's secretary and personal confidante was dispatched to New York to escort my friend to California for last-minute contract talks.

My friend, a very sensitive and aware woman, had an impression of danger from the day the secretary arrived in New York City.

"What is it you felt?" I later asked her.

"Just a sense of foreboding. Like I didn't want to go. Bad vibrations. Even on the day we were to leave, I really wanted to get out of it. In fact, I tried to find excuses not to leave."

My friend said that all went well enough on the trip to Kennedy Airport. Both women checked their baggage and were waiting for their boarding announcement when the secretary's name was announced over the loudspeaker, paging her for a phone call. The secretary went to the nearest telephone.

Much time passed and the secretary did not return. My friend made her way over to the telephone as the other passengers were boarding the plane. She found the secretary bent over the phone, immersed in a most difficult conversation, her voice filled with strain and emotion. Finally she hung up.

"What's the matter?" my friend asked.

The secretary told her that it was a phone call from the West Coast. The actress, her employer, was having a miscarriage.

My friend seized the opportunity to say that under the circumstances she would not go to California at that time, but would wait until the actress was fully recovered.

The secretary boarded the plane, leaving my much-relieved friend behind. But in the middle of the next night, my friend's telephone rang. It was the secretary.

"Please . . . help me . . . I need your help," came the frightened voice over the phone.

"Where are you?"

"I'm back at Kennedy Airport. I didn't know where else to go, whom to call. You were so kind to me when I was there, I took a plane back. I don't want to talk about this over the phone. Could you please come to the airport and get me?"

My friend explained the situation to her husband and they left to find the desperate woman. When they did locate her at the airport she was disheveled and appeared to have been beaten.

"My God, what has happened to you?" asked my friend.

"Well, I got off the plane in Los Angeles and took a cab to the house. Some strange woman came to the door and told me that my services were no longer needed. I insisted on seeing [actress's name] but they wouldn't let me into the house. I told them that I had news from New York for her and that my clothes and belongings were inside. I tried to enter. They began to push me and said the strangest thing. . . ."

At this point the woman became quite upset and started to cry.

My friend asked, "What was it they said?"

"They told me that she now *belonged* to them. That they were in charge of her comings and goings and that they alone would determine whom she was to see. There would be no negotiations, no contracts or business unless they deemed it so. She now belonged to them! Still, I insisted on seeing her. Then several of them pushed me into a car and drove off, out into the secluded California desert. There they forced me out of the car, broke beer bottles, and threatened to cut me up if I ever dared to show my face at the house again. They punched me a number of times and finally left me there. I have never been so frightened in my life . . . I didn't know what to do. . . ."

My friend and her husband took the near-hysterical woman back to their apartment and let her stay the night. She left the next day. They did not hear from her again.

It is highly probable that these girls who said they "owned" the actress were members of a drug-cult group. Many stories about this actress—her going off the deep end, steeping herself in the darker aspects of the occult, and keeping the company of very far-out friends—have been circulating for years. (In fact, during one appearance, accepting an award for a television show, she was noticeably under the influence of either drugs or hypnotism.)

Eileen Dent, a writer who has done some traveling with me gathering material for a biography on my life, recently told me the story of an occurrence that involved four young friends of her daughter who live in Los Angeles.

They were returning from a trip to San Francisco. As they rode, darkness descended. One of the quartet became quite uneasy and finally said that he wanted to get out of the car, that he would hitch a ride back to San Francisco. He was getting very bad vibrations. They pulled over and he got out.

The remaining three, one girl and two boys, drove a while longer and then decided to stop for the night. They liked the out-of-doors and had slept under the stars each night of the trip. Pitching a camp, with sleeping bags and a driftwood fire, they went to sleep.

Several hours later the two boys, who were about twenty feet away from the girl, were awakened by her screams. Jumping to their feet, they discovered that the girl was surrounded by a group of black-garbed and hooded persons. As they encircled her, the intruders chanted in low ominous tones which broke the silence in the dark night.

"Keep yelling," one of the boys called over to her, noticing that the louder the girl screamed, the more the hooded gang backed off.

Finally the strange intruders disappeared into the surrounding woods, and as they retreated one of them turned to the boys and said, "It's okay, we took your wallets while you slept, we have your names and addresses, and we'll get you yet!"

Scared out of their wits, the three of them scrambled their things together and dashed for the car. They drove as quickly as possible, until they reached their destination, the home of one of them. Unable to sleep, they huddled together in the living room, trying to talk one another out of the fear that had all but overcome them.

Toward morning the doorbell rang. It was the police, who had in tow the stray boy of the original quartet.

"Do you know this person?" a police officer asked them.

They told the officer that he was a friend of theirs.

"We found him wandering on the road, up in the hills. Says that he was with you, left the car on his own, got tired, and went to sleep. Says that he awakened to find some black-hooded people walking around him and singing. Says he barely escaped from them, left his things behind."

The now petrified three related their story to the police, who diligently took all the information down.

These four young people were indeed lucky. They apparently had been surrounded by one of the many black-cult groups that thrive in lower California. Many of these groups hold rituals that include human sacrifice. There are dozens of unsolved murders in California; cases of young girls who have been ritualistically murdered and decapitated. Hundreds upon hundreds of disemboweled animals have been found in the hills and on the beaches of California, evidence that they had been used in black art rituals.

One of the most prominent of the black-cult groups has several names, one being the "Church of the Final Judgment." The souls who join cults such as this, I believe, dwell in Darkness.

As reported in the November, 1972, issue of *Esquire*, this far-out "church" started in England in this century. The main precept of this secret organization is to aid and abet the end of the world by the use of violence and murder. The creation of chaos, personal and political, is its highest ideal. The general age of this so-called church's members is between eighteen and twenty-five.

In their extreme naïveté (a trait which appears to be a prerequisite for those who become members of such cults) these church members, like Charles Manson's group, believe that they are the chosen ones, that they alone will survive the oncoming destruction, which they feel is inevitable. Manson, by the way, took most of his tenets from this group's.

Along with other black-arts groups (such as the Solar Lodge of the Ordo Templi Orientis) they seem to be wreaking havoc not only in Los Angeles but in cities all over America. Modern black-art cults are into every form of evil—from black magic to voodoo to blood-drinking. By 1968 they were flourishing in the Santa Cruz Mountains of California and had established meeting places in Los Angeles, San Francisco, New York, and in major cities of Europe as well.

Most of these groups, which happen to be almost 100 percent white, hate the black race; and the way, they feel, that world chaos can be brought to immediate fruition is to incite whites against blacks into an all-out war (another case of naïveté, for how can they possibly believe that, in a civil war in the United States between blacks and whites, they would be spared by the blacks whom they so hate?).

It is most interesting to note here that very few black persons in America become involved in black magic or the occult. In my investigations I have discovered that a possible reason for their keeping clear of occult teachings is that many blacks feel that this would be taking a step backward in their present rapid climb up the social, economic, and political ladders.

Many of the teachings of black magic came out of black-populated countries, such as those located in Africa and the Caribbean. And, almost without exception, there is a tendency for blacks in the United States to keep a far distance from anything which might connect them with rituals or superstitions, those things which at one time were deeply a part of their ancestors' cultures.

Persons belonging to black-arts churches were seen in full public view, on the streets of southern-California communities, black hoods and all, until the murder of Robert Kennedy, which just happened to occur in Los Angeles. They then seemed to vanish from sight.

A strange set of what intellectual minds will undoubtedly call "coincidences" surround the Robert Kennedy case. The facts are:

1. Many black-art California-based cults such as the Church of the Final Judgment teach the destruction of the United States through chaos and mass violence.

2. Members of these cults generally hate blacks.

3. Robert Kennedy worked for the advancement of blacks and was generally liked, trusted, and respected by them.

4. Black art cults are mainly localized in the Los Angeles area.

5. Robert Kennedy was assassinated in Los Angeles.

6. Sirhan Sirhan, the assassin of Robert Kennedy, had studied mysticism and was a devotee (albeit a misguided one) of Mme. Blavatsky, the woman who founded the Theosophical Society, and many of whose beliefs were not only mystically but politically inspired as well. (While living in India, she openly denounced the pacifist ways of Mahatma Gandhi, who was himself eventually assassinated!)

7. Charles Manson, while in prison in the nineteen-sixties, had also studied the occult teachings of Mme. Blavatsky, along with those of other mystical personalities.

8. The night before Robert Kennedy was murdered he had his last dinner with Sharon Tate and her husband, Roman Polanski.

9. A few months later, Sharon Tate and her friends were killed by Charles Manson's family.

One of the most interesting aspects of the Robert Kennedy assassination was the initial report that when Kennedy's bodyguard, Rosy Grier, a strapping, massive ex-football player, tried to wrest the gun from Sirhan Sirhan's grasp, there had been quite a struggle. In fact, more bullets were fired into the air during this time. Grier finally had to smash the killer's hand against a kitchen wall and almost crush it with his foot before the death weapon was released. Sirhan is extremely small, an underweight and weakly person. A psychiatrist's report in the Los Angeles *Times* stated that there was only one explanation for Sirhan Sirhan's iron grip on the pistol—he was under the influence of hypnotism, either self-induced or directed from an outside force.

Sirhan Sirhan apparently did not feel any of the pain that had been inflicted on him, or he would have dropped the gun much sooner than he did; he had, I believe, been hypnotized.

I am not a fanatic and have not conjured up some sensational fantasy to pass off as truth. As far back as 1965 I knew that Robert Kennedy would be assassinated if he went toward the White House. On the evening of December 27, 1967, on an NBC radio program, "The Long John Nebel Show," I was asked who would be running in the next election. I said Nixon and Humphrey.

"And what about Robert Kennedy?" my host asked.

"There will never be another Kennedy in the White House" was my reply.

"He will at least run."

"I don't think so."

At that time, in 1967, Kennedy was the most promising Democratic hopeful. It seemed, from a political standpoint at least, that he indeed would be a nominee. Some of the other guests on the program argued with me that Robert Kennedy had to be the man nominated by the Democrats. Others even wanted to bet me huge sums of money.

"There will never be another Kennedy in the White House," I reiterated, wishing to leave it at that.

I no longer make assassination predictions over the airwaves, fully realizing their suggestion potential to someone with the desire to fulfill a prediction made by a well-known psychic. But, off the air I said that I felt if Robert Kennedy did go for the White House he would be murdered, as his brother was.

Privately, with my students and in small groups, I had asked that good vibrations, prayers, and thoughts be sent to the Kennedys, for the evil forces were bent on destroying them and would utilize anyone who aligned himself with Darkness to accomplish the task.

I do feel that evil forces have spread across the country. There is a saying that any new concept, whether it be fashion, fad, or teaching, comes from the West Coast. In my autobiography, *The Reluctant Prophet*, published in 1968, I spoke of my experiences in Los Angeles when I was there in 1966. The vibrations of that city disturbed me. I could not do psychic work. I could not meditate. There was a deadness, a horrible feeling of doom in the very smog-ridden air I breathed. It wasn't half as bad when I went to San Francisco soon thereafter.

Only a few years have passed since that time, and the negativism I felt in Los Angeles has now become widespread throughout the country. Presently, New York City has even more evil vibrations than Los Angeles. The black-arts and devious-cult groups have taken a plague-like grip on large sections of our society. Pick up any underground newspaper—and some not so underground, especially in New York City—and you will find ads for lectures, seminars, and personal instruction in the various black arts. The stores are filled with books on everything from How to Become a Witch to How to Destroy Those You Don't Like by the Use of Voodoo. Television has taken up the call; no less than five films made expressly for television with plot lines involving black magic or cultism of some sort have been aired in the week that I am writing this. And this is in addition to two weekly series that deal with the Darker, more horrendous aspects of the occult.

I am frightened. The powers of Darkness are gaining

much influence over the people of our country. The harmless interest in astrology and reincarnation has grown into a mass curiosity about evil. Many young people are innocently—some not so innocently—becoming victims of devil worship. And as it looks now, several prospective leaders of our country may be more involved in the black arts than is publicly known at the present time.

I psychically feel that there is a direct connection with the Dark powers of the occult and the assassinations of both the Kennedys and Martin Luther King. Their murderers had each delved into the baser teachings of occultism and mysticism.

The Devil walked out of California and across the country and is now gathering recruits for the most devious work—the destruction of the United States.

I am not a prophet of doom, nor do I have any axe to grind. I certainly am not an overreligious, crusading zealot, as I do not have a religious affiliation at this time. But my psychic sense is overwhelmed by the evil in the atmosphere which prevails throughout many of our towns and cities.

The imminent destruction of Los Angeles and other sections of California by earthquake, which many psychics, including myself, have predicted for years, will be an actual happening, because the majority of the people do not turn to the Light. As I stated earlier, evil does eventually destroy itself and those who join forces with it. I firmly believe that in certain instances even an earthquake can be brought about by the evil thoughts of man.

When the earthquake occurs, a vast change in thinking will take place in the United States. I have found in my travels that the Orientals and those who live in the Mideast reach for spiritual Light more than their Western counterparts. One reason is that they know what it is like to live with the possibility of losing hundreds of thousands of lives in a single catastrophe, whether it be earthquake, typhoon, or atomic weapons.

Let us hope that an event such as a major earthquake will not have to be the instrument to wake up the spiritually dormant or the evil-seeking souls of this great country.

CHAPTER 2

Neam! Livee morf su revilled tub
Noishaytpmet ootni ton suh deel
Suh tshaiga sapsert tath yeth
Vigrawf eu za sesapsert rua suh viegrawf
Derb ilaid rua yed sith suh vig

Neveh ni si za thre ni
Nud eebliw eyth
Much mod-ngik eyth
Main eyth eeb dwohlah
Neveh ni tra chico
Rertharf rua!

WHAT YOU HAVE JUST READ IS THE LORD'S PRAYER, WRITten backward. It has been written phonetically, and its recital is the first step to take in the utilization of witchcraft, one of the darker constituents of evil. Said backward, the Lord's Prayer is supposed to help one throw off all previous "religious, national and political cant" and bring one closer to the forces of the Devil; or so teaches one of its practitioners who has recently come into fame because of his dealings in witchcraft.

The Lord's Prayer symbolizes Good. Its feeling is positive and is filled with compassion for the soul. Most importantly, it offers a protection against the Dark forces, especially when the words "deliver us from evil" are spoken.

Reciting the Lord's Prayer backward seems childish and inane. But the motivations for doing so are fraught with ill will and egregiousness.

The book from which I extracted this initial lesson in deviltry literally pulsates with evil intent. (It was a best seller of sorts for the author, a professed "black witch.") Let me but list the chapter headings so that you may judge for yourself.

Vengeance and Attack
The Coven and How to Form One
Counter Magic
Spells

The most disquieting ideas in this book come under the heading of "Curses." This chapter actually instructs the reader in how to "do in" those he thinks he needs to destroy or control. It explains in minute detail how a person, through the use of witchcraft, can bend the mind and will of others.

Karma, a concept usually found in teachings of the occult, is not once taken into consideration here. One is supposed to forge ahead in life making those he comes in contact with submit to his will. If a person chooses not to love you . . . simply put a love spell on him. Sigmund Freud said that it is easy to bend the subconscious will of those who are not armed against the onslaught of evil sent into the atmosphere by telepathy.

Throughout most of my life I have been repelled by witchcraft. I have been fascinated by it, but for some reason never involved myself in its manifestations. Although I have investigated almost every aspect of the occult, the world of the witch has been the one I purposefully avoided. It was only recently that a series of events occurred which made me understand why I felt this repulsion and fear.

In order to appreciate and understand these incidents it is necessary for you to know that I firmly believe in reincarnation. While I was in the Orient, several things happened to me that proved I had lived a previous life in Japan. These occurrences are detailed in an earlier book, *Your Eastern Star.*

The strongest evidence was during my visit to the remote, sacred island of Miya-jima, which lies in the southern inland sea of that country. For a period of six hours or more I experienced *déjà vu,* wherein I was able to take my guide and interpreter around the island, having total recall of pathways, roads, houses, temples, and the natural settings which abound on that mysterious lovely island.

I had been able to follow every turn on the twisting dirt roads of Miya-jima, fully knowing what was around each bend long before I took the turn. It was as though a map had been laid out in my head, more likely that I had been there before, in another lifetime, and was remembering that time. This occurrence and many others, such as my ability to pick up the Japanese language instantly, and not only to understand but to conform to difficult Japanese traditions and customs, proved to me that I had indeed been reincarnated.

In 1971 I was asked to lecture to a Spiritual Frontiers

group in upstate New York, on the campus of a famous college. While there I stayed at the home of one of the group who was in charge of bringing lecturers to the city. I'll call her Jane, an attractive thirtyish housewife. She is of the Roman Catholic faith and has one child.

She had originally heard of me through an article which had been published in a local newspaper. She had written to me requesting a psychic consultation, a professional service of mine. When she had arrived at my office, we had sensed a fine rapport with each another. We had had that somewhat discomforting feeling of having met before.

The college lecture was a success, and I remained at Jane's house for several days giving consultations. The longer I stayed in her home, the stronger the feeling was that Jane and I had somehow known each other before—perhaps in another life, or so we speculated. Occasionally we called each other by different names. I referred to her several times as Jenny, and she addressed me as John. Jane's sense of humor fit right in with mine, and we kidded each other upon the first day of my arrival, as a brother and sister might tease each other.

Eileen Dent had accompanied me to this city, in order to watch me under fire and gather more material for her book about me. Jane was most anxious for the three of us to use her Ouija board. I declined several times, stating that although I did not disbelieve that anything truly psychic could occur with a Ouija board, the results were not reliable; for an individual's subconscious can move the planchette as well as any outside force. The information gleaned from the board can thus prove to be dangerous.

"Come on," Jane said. "I have a feeling it will be a terrific experience."

"Go ahead," said Eileen, an absolute nonbeliever in the

board. "It'll be a good change from the exhausting readings you've been giving."

One evening I reluctantly gave in to their prodding. Jane's husband was away on business and her son, Edward, was put to bed. The date was September 15, 1971. The time was between ten and eleven-thirty.

The Ouija board was set up on the kitchen table. Jane sat opposite me, Eileen to my right. Placing our hands on the planchette, Jane and I were surprised to find immediate movement. We accused each other of manipulating it. Eileen, skeptical and practical-thinking as ever, laughed. The planchette moved at top speed, making small circles on the board. My fingers barely touched the small object, and at times the planchette would get away from us completely, skittering across the table onto the floor.

"Ask it something," Eileen insisted, pen and notebook in hand, ready to take down any given information, whether it be conjured, subconscious, or otherwise.

"Are there any spirits present?" I asked, half jokingly.

The planchette spelled out the letters YES.

"Identify yourself," Eileen demanded.

BOB WIDDENFIELD, spelled out by the planchette. It sped to the numerals *1696*—a figure we took to be a date.

The following is a direct transcript of the shorthand notes Eileen took that evening. It was difficult for her to keep up with the movement of the planchette, as it literally took off on its own; Jane and I were flabbergasted by its speed.

QUESTION: You say that your name is Bob Widdenfield? Is that correct?

THE BOARD: Yes.

QUESTION: Did Eileen know you?

THE BOARD: No.
QUESTION: Did Daniel know you?
THE BOARD: Yes.
QUESTION: Where did you live?
THE BOARD: Salem.
QUESTION: In Massachusetts?
THE BOARD: Yes.
QUESTION (Jane): Was Daniel my brother?
THE BOARD: Yes.
QUESTION: What was our last name?
THE BOARD: Sherrwood
QUESTION: Is that the correct spelling?
THE BOARD: Old language.
QUESTION: Was Daniel's first name John?
THE BOARD: No. Second name John.
QUESTION: What was his first name?
THE BOARD: William.
QUESTION (Eileen): Did we call him John?
THE BOARD: Not we.
QUESTION (Jane): Did I call him John?
THE BOARD: Yes.
QUESTION: What was Jane's name in that life?
THE BOARD: Alice.
QUESTION (Jane): Did I have another name?
THE BOARD: Yes. Jennifer . . . Alice Jennifer.
QUESTION (Daniel): Why do we remember John and Jennifer [Jenny]? Why did we call each other by our middle names?
THE BOARD: Black women made you call each other that.
QUESTION: Why?
THE BOARD: A secret cult.
QUESTION (Eileen, now caught up in the intrigue of the story, if not the means of its telling): What secret cult?

THE BOARD: No. Shut up, Eileen. Too fast. Too fast.

There was a pause and then the planchette spelled out I AM A DISCARNATE, PRAY FOR ME—PLEASE. We stopped for a moment and did say a prayer of sorts.

THE BOARD: John—John—Finnaly—old language—Finnaly killed Jennifer.
QUESTION: How old was he when he killed her?
THE BOARD: Eighteen.
QUESTION: Why did he kill her?
THE BOARD: He wanted to break the spell—partly—black spell broken. Black women put spell. Witches.
QUESTION (Jane): Why did he kill me?
THE BOARD: They used you both in rituals.
QUESTION: Why did Daniel [John] kill Jane [Jennifer]?
THE BOARD: She loved John, incestuously. John wanted to break spell.
QUESTION (Jane): How did he kill me?
THE BOARD: Yes. Fire. Not at the stake. Home. Burned in house.

At this point, Jane and I looked at each other in amazement. We are both petrified of fire and smoke, and voiced this only now after the board spelled out how I (John) had killed her (Jennifer) in Salem so long ago.

QUESTION (asked by Jane for a reason I suspect she felt within): Was there anyone else killed?
THE BOARD: Edward. Your son, Edward.
QUESTION (Jane): Who was Edward then?
THE BOARD: Your father.

I must digress here for a moment. When Jane had first come to me for her private consultation we talked about her son, who was barely three at the time. Without getting any clue as to their relationship, I psychically perceived that Edward was going to give Jane a most difficult time. I told her that the vibrations of the child seemed far beyond his years and that in many ways he acted like an adult.

I recall saying, "As soon as Edward can talk he will dictate to you, more like a father than a son." Jane had been amazed at my perception, for apparently the child had already taken to such tactics. The Ouija board seemed to be fitting many pieces together, unless one of our subconscious minds was strong enough to energize it.

Meanwhile, back at the planchette . . .

QUESTION: Did John mean to kill Jennifer?
THE BOARD: Yes. He felt the only way to break the evil spell.
QUESTION: Did he mean to kill his father?
THE BOARD: No. Herman was Edward's name then.

For some reason, the name Herman as applied to that small child asleep upstairs struck me as funny, and I laughed.

THE BOARD: Don't play games about this.
QUESTION: How old was John when he died?
THE BOARD: Fifty-six.
QUESTION (Daniel): How did I die?
THE BOARD: Suicide. Fire—suffered guilt, then burned himself.
QUESTION (Daniel): Is that why, above all else, I am afraid of fire?
THE BOARD: Yes.
QUESTION (Jane): Was it a painful death?
THE BOARD: Yes.
QUESTION: Was Jennifer used in the cult?
THE BOARD: Yes. She liked it.

QUESTION (Eileen): Exactly how were John and Jennifer used in this witches' cult?
THE BOARD: Sexually . . . sex rituals . . . black magic.

Out of complete embarrassment in front of Jane and Eileen, I immediately changed the subject and asked the supposed Bob Widdenfield if he liked Eileen.

YES, the planchette pointed out.

QUESTION: Does Eileen like you?
THE BOARD: Shit. She does not believe.

Then the board spelled out the words THIS IS NOT EVIL. WHAT IS EVIL?

Before we could continue questioning, the board gave a message to Eileen, as if to prove the validity of the Ouija to her. It said her daughter, Karen, who was home in New York City, was going through a rough time: KAREN DENT WILL HAVE A BAD EXPERIENCE TONIGHT AND THAT WILL PROVE MY [Bob Widdenfield's] EXISTENCE. NOT TOO BAD, KAREN IS PHYSICALLY ALL RIGHT. (The next day Eileen called her home and found that Karen had spent a bad night with their pet dog, Susie, who had had a heart attack.)

At this point, Jane left the kitchen and went upstairs to see if Edward was all right. Eileen said that she would like to take Jane's place on the board while she was gone.

Eileen moved over to Jane's seat and touched the planchette. Before I could place my fingers on it, the planchette suddenly flew across the Ouija board, leapt in the air, and struck Eileen in the chest.

I have never seen anyone so startled in my life. Eileen shrieked, fully comprehending that the planchette had taken off on its own. Her laugh was nearly hysterical and the tears began to roll down her cheeks. She was really quite upset. The skeptic, the complete nonbeliever in the Ouija board, had sat to "play a game" and the game had actually turned on her. I was quite smugly delighted.

The Ouija board incident appeared, on the surface at least, to be fascinating and yet, still, not entirely credible. But the denouement, which was to take place a few nights later, was something out of an Alfred Hitchcock or Rod Serling television script.

It was on the evening before I was to leave for my New York City home. To reciprocate their hospitality, I had decided to take Jane and her husband, who had returned from his trip, to dinner. Eileen accompanied us as well. On the way to the restaurant, we dropped Edward off at a friend's house.

During dinner, Jane and I had continued our "sibling" teasing of each other. One of the items on the menu was a flaming shish kebab. I had used that as a starting point for several jokes about burning and Salem.

After dinner, we picked up Edward. It was very late when we did this and Edward was physically worn out from a long day's activities. He put his head down in his mother's lap and fell asleep.

Eileen and I were in the back seat. Jane was in front, her husband driving, with Edward between them.

While we were driving home, I took out a match, feigned lighting it, and threw it at Jane. She was about to respond when Edward, whose head had been face down and who could not physically have seen what was happening, sat up in the seat. Groggy-eyed, half asleep, almost semitrancelike, he turned his little body around to face me and said, "Are you going to burn my mommy again?"

Eileen and I turned to each other. The astounding confirmation in his statement, verifying the words brought to us by the Ouija, left us speechless. We assured him that I would not.

"Then what are your 'tentions?" the three-year-old demanded, in a fatherly tone.

"I love your mother," I said. "I wouldn't want to hurt her . . . I love her."

"Then are you going to burn me?" Edward asked in a very frightened voice.

"Never! I love you!" I replied, very shaken.

Reassured, Edward put his head back down and once again fell asleep.

We talked about this latest development in the story of Edward, Jane, and me—at one time a father and two children. Edward's room was upstairs, not over the kitchen. When we had used the Ouija board, there had been two doors—both closed—and a long hallway between us and the child. There was no way that Edward could have heard us. We had made sure that we did not discuss anything pertaining to the supposed past life in Salem in front of him, knowing that it could possibly upset him. And he had been sound asleep when Jane had gone up to check on him.

The only explanation for his exclamation in the car was that, the moment he awakened, he had been able to reach into his subconscious where, if one goes deep enough, incidents of a past life can be recalled.

The fear that was evident in this child's voice was far beyond that justified by anything he could possibly have overheard. He mentioned it again, just that once in the trancelike state he appeared in during the car ride. His few words and his apprehension then seemed to confirm the story that Jane and I had indeed known each other in a past life and that we had participated in a black-magic cult.

It was quite a while before I got over the experience

of that visit to upstate New York and the happenings that occurred in Jane's house. The incidents were so very revealing and shocking to each of us that their ramifications are still being felt. Much time has elapsed since my visit, and I have been told that Edward has further developed paternalistic feelings toward Jane and expresses himself quite freely to her as a father would, rather than a son.

There have been times when I have been able to tune into that life when I was "evil." However, it is still much too painful, and I have been avoiding "going back" too deeply for that reason. Eventually I would like to work with a hypnotist and have him regress me to that time, an exploration that could be most helpful in understanding my karmic destiny in this present life.

Another recent happening that makes me think about the possibility of my having dealt in witchcraft in previous lives involves cats.

Although I have had every other kind of pet in my life, until a few years ago I never had a cat. It is the one animal for which I have had a distinct dislike since childhood—almost a kind of fear.

In 1968, I bought a small house in upstate New York. One day while antique hunting, I pulled my car up in front of an old, barnlike building that had been converted into an antique shop. As I was standing on the porch, looking over some old wooden benches, a gray late-model car drove up in the semicircular driveway. The car slowed, a lady rolled down the window and threw a brown paper bag onto the sidewalk in front of the building. The car then sped off.

I looked down at the bag and noticed movement. I reached down and opened it, and out came a small, adorable kitten. The antique dealer, who had also seen the incident, came out of the shop, reached down, and picked up the frightened animal.

Looking it over, he said, "Dammit, it's a female. Lousy summer people come up here with their animals and some of them have babies, which they then proceed to get rid of before taking off for their city homes again. I'll call the ASPCA right away."

"What will they do with it?" I asked.

"Well, it's a female, so they'll probably put it to sleep. Too many cats up here already."

"No," I said, hating to hear of any animal being put to sleep. "I'll take it, I'll find a home for it."

I took the kitten home, not at all intending to keep it. However, after the first few days, I was hooked. She immediately made friends with my other pets—Bambi (a Chihuahua), Toro (a domesticated robin), and an unnamed rabbit. And she adored me. The kitten was lovely. She had a darker surface coat of gray with lighter gray fur beneath. She looked like velvet, especially in the light, which would heighten the two shades. When I took her to the vet, I discovered that she was almost a purebred Burmese.

She had the most striking deep-yellow eyes. Mischief was her second name. Because of this and her penetrating eyes, I named her Rosemary, after the mother in the book *Rosemary's Baby*. On an outward, conscious level, I did not connect her with any kind of witchcraft, other than her appearance, which somehow brought to mind the description of the devil-baby in the book.

When I went to the Orient, I placed Rosemary with my mother. Months later, upon my return, I found that my mother had renamed the kitten. She is a very religious Catholic and just didn't like the implications of calling the kitten Rosemary, or so she explained. But my mother is very psychic and probably sensed something more, as she had not even read *Rosemary's Baby.* Having known that Mia Farrow played in the film version, my mother had decided to call the kitten Mia. I think she felt that I wouldn't be quite so upset by the sudden change if the new name was somehow related to the old reason I had named the kitten Rosemary.

I didn't object. In fact, Mia was easier to say than Rosemary, and I had gotten into the habit of calling her Rose when I was angry with her, a name I detest for anything other than the flower.

After I returned from the Orient, I got a large dog for my country home. He was an Alaskan malamute, weighing about one hundred pounds. I named him Yuki, which means snow in Japanese.

Yuki was a mere puppy when I acquired him and he got along famously with Mia and the other animals. Mia had a great interest in stalking Yuki and making him chase her. She loved to stand up on her hind legs and box Yuki's long snout.

About a year later, I was called away on some business and left Mia with my parents. This time, a group of neighborhood children took to some evil doings on their own. They were feeding poisoned tidbits to the cats in the community. Mia, unfortunately, was a victim. I was horrified when my mother described the slow, painful death that Mia suffered. Distraught, I vowed never to have a cat again. Even my own family cannot believe what happened next—within two months of Mia's death.

I have an office in New York City, where I give psychic consultations, and I decided to move it from the building where I was into another location. It took months to find a place that I could use as an office and also as an apartment to stay in when I did not go to my country house.

A friend, Barbara Weprin, who is psychically aware,

one day recommended that I come up to where she lived, near Riverside Drive on the West Side of New York, to see if I liked her building. It was a nice old building and was rent-controlled.

It was a lovely day, bright and smogless, and I asked Barbara if she would like to go for a walk along the park on Riverside Drive. We had just crossed over into Riverside Park when Barbara said, "Stop a minute, what's that noise? Sounds like a hurt animal."

The crying of an animal could be heard quite clearly, and we traced it to the entrance of the West Side Highway, which runs between the park and the Hudson River. An animal was about to run out onto the highway. I hopped over the barrier, dashed across the two-lane parkway, and scooped the animal up in my hands.

Before I could get a good look at it, Barbara, who had caught up with me, pointed at the kitten in disbelief. "Daniel!" she exclaimed. "It's Mia!"

There in my hands was the exact same cat I had once owned, the only difference being that it was a kitten. A female kitten. Exactly the same two tones of gray, a combination I have not seen before or since, the penetrating deep-yellow eyes, the lack of any other markings—it was Mia in miniature.

"Let's take it to some cat shelter, or ask someone to keep it as a pet."

"I really think you should keep it, Daniel," Barbara said. "It was meant for you to have, it's too much of a coincidence." After great deliberation, and after trying to get rid of it, I took it home and adopted it.

There was no other name for it but Mia, and she is now called Mia II. Yuki, who hated all cats except the original Mia, whom he grew up with, did not sense that Mia II was a different animal. He took to her as if she indeed was the first cat, and now they play together in the same way. And the kitten had no fear of Yuki, who is about fifty times bigger than she is.

When I took Mia II to my house in the country, she walked into the kitchen, sniffed around a bit, then walked through the living room, turned the corner leading to the stairway, and went upstairs. Out of all the rooms she could have chosen, she picked the one I sleep in, went in, looked at both beds, picked out mine, jumped on it, curled up, and went to sleep. Mia I always loved to curl up in the same manner during the day.

On my round oak kitchen table, I keep a most unusually large bowl, ceramic and handmade. Mia I for some strange reason loved to come into the kitchen, jump onto the table, and try to fit into the bowl, making a complete circle around the bottom of it with her body. On the first day that Mia II was in my home she did precisely the same thing. It was uncanny, as if Mia I had never left. In fact, Mia II is so similar to Mia I that I sometimes forget that Mia II is really a different cat—physically at least.

When I had been searching out my own life's pattern, back in the late nineteen-fifties and early 'sixties, I used to go to Room 1010 at Carnegie Hall, a room located in the complex of offices, living quarters, singing studios, and dance-rehearsal rooms above Carnegie Hall. Room 1010 was actually a Spiritualist church of sorts, and every Wednesday at two o'clock I would traipse up there and let the resident medium give me guidance and tell me of my future.

This lady would sit on an old, elaborately carved mahogany chair. She was part black and part Spanish. There was an unfathomable look in her eyes and she was indeed psychic, having told me several things which came out as she predicted—some only now, almost fifteen years later, are being verified or can be interpreted in relation to my life.

The Mia incident prompted me to go through the dozens of notebooks that I keep on psychic happenings. I was looking for the notebooks on Room 1010, Carnegie Hall, as I dimly recalled something about cats that had upset me back then. I found them.

"Why are you afraid of cats?" the medium had asked me during one of the readings.

"I just don't particularly like cats," I said, or so the notebook states. "I'm not afraid of them."

"Yes, you are. That's why you don't have any," she said. The medium always went into a trance when she worked—head bowed, voice heavy, hands jerking about from time to time. "You will have a cat someday, the same cat you had in another life. It will come to you, and when it does you will understand."

Mediums are always saying that when the projected occurrence happens one will understand. I used to think it was a cop-out.

The medium continued, "You had this animal in another life. You performed something bad . . . it was not a good experience."

"I love animals. I would never hurt an animal," I protested.

"You didn't hurt the animal. The evil you did was with and through the cat. She was your familiar in another life. . . ."

"What's that? What's a familiar?" I demanded, by now quite irritated by the prospect of having to contend with an animal I am not at all fond of.

"I cannot take the time to tell you. You will look it up, research it, and then you will understand."

Again the "understand" bit, I thought.

At the time I was going to the medium my work was

in the theater and writing. I had never dreamed of becoming a professional psychic. Instead of telling me about my show-business career, this woman was wasting my time with stories about cats.

"When the cat comes to you in this life, it will be a symbol that you are using your abilities in the correct way this time, not as you had done in another life."

Mumbo jumbo, I thought. I went out of Room 1010 quite angry that day. Some time later, I decided to check out what she meant by "familiar."

Much to my horror, I found that familiars, according to the occult dictionaries I searched through, are the errand runners and advisors of witches. After making a pact with evil, a witch is granted the company of an animal by the Devil. It is usually a small domestic animal, one that can be kept in the house, such as a cat, dog, toad, or sometimes a bird. There are accounts of witches using familiars for all sorts of mayhem they wish to perpetrate on others, including murder. Reginald Scot, in a book on witchcraft published in 1584, named the animals that witches usually keep "familiars," or "familiar spirits."

When I discovered what the word meant and thought about the implications of what the medium had said, I was infuriated. The audacity of her even suggesting such an untruth! In this life I had never tried to use any form of power, good or evil, for self gain.

However, as time passed I became more involved in psychic work—especially through my own meditations—and aware of why this very pronounced psychic ability was given to me in this life. The Ouija-board incident proved, to me at least, that in past lives I had misused my psychic power for my own selfish ends and I had hurt many souls. In this life the power that I had developed in previous lives was given to me at birth. It was the working out of a karmic debt—something I had utilized for evil in the past would now be put to the test in the present life. I again had the choice to use that power for good or evil. Fortunately, I can honestly say that I have tried to use it only for the good of others and their advancement, psychically or spiritually, although there have been times of great temptation and near-catastrophes.

I have received Mia twice. No one can tell me that Mia II isn't Mia I. Many acquaintances who didn't see me between the time that Mia I died and Mia II took her place say that it *is* the same cat. My parents know the story is true, for they had Mia I buried. And Barbara Weprin knows, as she was with me when I "found" Mia II. It is a bit uncanny and if I didn't understand the spiritual ramifications, I would be quite, as the saying goes, freaked out by this.

When I took Mia II to my parents' home, all my doubt about the validity of this unusual reincarnation incident vanished. Mia II is a most calm, playful, trusting, and altogether friendly animal. When she first arrived at my parents' house, she acted altogether different from the animal she was. I carried her into the kitchen from the garage, where I had parked my car. As I opened the door to the house, Mia II leapt out of my arms, her fur standing on end. A growl that sounded as if she were being tortured emanated from her. She raced upstairs and, finding one of the bedrooms empty, scurried under the bed. It took me a good fifteen minutes to get her out of the hiding place.

Mia II has visited other homes and never acts in the manner she does whenever she is at my parents'. She attacks everyone who comes near her, grabbing a leg with her front paws and trying to bite. She is clearly afraid when she takes to employing these protective tactics. It is as if she has complete recall of having been hurt in that house. The madness that overtakes her disappears the moment we leave. The whole family is kind to Mia II—in fact, they tend to act overkindly, to win her over. But she will have none of it. She hisses, growls, and attacks any and all moving objects there.

Mia II remembers having died in that house and she wants nothing to do with it. Even my parents, very skeptical in these matters, now believe that Mia II does recall something that happened to her when she was Mia I.

My abhorrence and hatred of black-art witchcraft probably stem from the fact that in past lives I *was* a witch and did much harm, and that subconsciously I remember it. I have not yet discovered what I did in Salem after murdering my sister (now Jane) and my father (now Edward). The Ouija board says that I lived until I was fifty-six and then committed suicide. There were many years in between and I will not meditate on them, for I can sense that there was much evil in that life. It could very easily have been the time I had used Mia as a familiar.

CHAPTER 3

Black magic or devil worship is the use of supernatural knowledge for the purpose of evil. It is the conjuring forth of diabolic and hellish forces that become emissaries and subjects of those who would utilize them.

Throughout history, when these forces are used for ill, they have been known to cause havoc and destruction. Black magic has inflicted disease and even death on those on whom its practitioners have decided to unleash their powers.

Black magicians are much like their counterparts—those persons who seek the Light through either religion, yoga, or other self-taught and -imposed disciplines—in that they usually hold ceremonies, say prayers, commit themselves to ritual, undergo fasts, and believe in a force that is not of earthly confines. The similarity ends there. Black magicians and their advocates make animal and sometimes human sacrifices, teach the appeasement of human desires through complete participation in their rituals, and stop at nothing to bring about chaos and destruction to the laws of the land, the laws of nature, the laws of the universe. In so doing, they seek advancement for themselves and their evil cause. Persons who align themselves with evil believe that the force will grant them any desire.

Interest in and worship of unseen forces can be traced back to prehistoric times. Writings and drawings on cave walls indicate that early man believed in and revered a horned god—a human form dressed in animal skins and antlers. Our concept of the Devil as a horned, hooved being with a tail is mostly derived from these early cave paintings, or so believes the archaeologist Margaret Murray.

Paleolithic man did not differentiate between a good and evil God. He believed that all things came from one God, that positive and negative forces were one. As man progressed, he discovered that the good force was indeed separate from the evil force. Devil-worshiping cults, along with positive religions, sprang up in early societies and spread throughout Europe, reaching a pinnacle in the Middle Ages. In these medieval times, the concepts of good and evil had been completely separated, and each had its own adherents. Paganism disappeared as the ancient gods became devils in the minds of the practitioners of evil. The ancient mysteries became orgies and their worship was termed sorcery.

Europe was a hotbed of evil worship in medieval times. Spain held the most adherents, with France running a close second. Devil worship was at this time helped along by those who did not truly believe in its power but merely used it as a means to advance their own political or religious ends. There were those who only wanted to satisfy base cravings by cheating, trickery, and mocking others. Many religious leaders of the day went far by accusing and condemning others of devil worship, most of them innocent victims. Unknowingly, these "witch hunters" were affording evil powers a chance to take hold, a hold that has not to this day been eliminated. Interesting, how evil will utilize those who either do not believe in it or make light of its power.

Spells were cast, hypnotism became widespread, the atmosphere of the Middle Ages breathed evil. As interest in and usage of the black arts spread and grew, there was a counterreaction. Some learned men did not wish to use magical powers for their own evil advancement. They reasoned that black-art rituals and practices could be harnessed to protect themselves and others from any evil that might be directed at them. This was the birth of white magic, a true antidote to the powers of darkness. Incantations against evil, exorcisms, amulets and talismans of precious stones, special potions came into use by those who wished to turn the evil force against itself.

Herbs and then chemicals as curatives were first introduced by those persons who practiced early forms of white magic in order to refute and lessen the potency of evil which so permeated the Middle Ages. Modern-day science owes much to these men who sought to counteract the diabolism of that era.

Sybil Leek, America's most famous witch, and a personal friend of mine, is the best example today of someone who uses white magic. Sybil does much good with her powers, seeking to assist those who come to her in need.

When I was stricken by a recurring gall-bladder disorder, Sybil was able to help me when physicians could not. She prescribed a potion made of five uncommon herbs, plus a short daily ritual. It did the trick. The pain and discomfort began to subside, and I was able to continue my work, something I had not been able to do after taking all the drugs administered to me by more scientific men.

White-magic practitioners believe that their power comes from the beneficent forces of nature. They use this power to heal and to do good for others. They also cast defensive spells against their counterparts, the black magicians. Those persons who delve into the black arts set out to invoke and manipulate power from the Darker forces of nature. A white magician never uses power for evil purpose or gain.

Sybil Leek considers her witchcraft a religion, one called "Wicca." Wiccas were early medieval medicine men.

"In pure witchcraft," says Sybil, "which is the religion of Wicca, the life force is of most importance. Wicca is a religion which preserves, protects, and strengthens life. Satanism is death."

The word *devil* is a derivation of the Greek word *diabolos,* which literally translated means "slanderer." It has come to represent the supreme spirit of evil, the enemy of God and man.

Satan is a Hebrew word, used by early Jews to name an angelic entity whose function it was to test man's fidelity to God. Both Job and Jesus in the wilderness were tested by Satan. Originally, Satan was not evil, but became evil by identification with his functions. It was not until the era of the New Testament that the word *Satan* became synonymous with *devil*, an enemy of God.

Lucifer, first to be invoked in the litanies of the witches' Sabbath, is said to have been an angel of God who fell from grace. Early Christian priests and scribes taught that Lucifer was a prince among angels, the wisest of all the angels, and perfect in beauty. They felt that Lucifer was actually the younger son of Jehovah. Legend has it that Lucifer led a rebellion against Jehovah. Michael, who was in command of the loyal angels, defeated the rebels and drove them out of heaven.

Jehovah supposedly gave Lucifer the earth to rule over. In Matthew 4:9 Satan says to Jesus, "All these things I will give thee, if thou wilt fall down and worship me." This offer, many believe, would not have been possible were the earth not Lucifer's to give. Those persons who are advocates of Satanism believe that the earth is the Devil's domain, and that if he is properly approached by them, he will afford them any of their worldly wishes or desires.

The Christian Church took up the fight against the Devil—giving him an identity, a history, and even a physical form. The Church of the Middle Ages gave us our concept of how the Devil supposedly looks. The pursuit of the Devil became a means of political advancement in the religious hierarchy. Accusations of devil worship were flung right and left. Countless hundreds of thousands of innocent people suffered torture and death in purges meant to cleanse the earth of the evil forces. Had our forefathers used a quarter of this righteous energy to honestly investigate evil rather than to make dishonest accusations, they might have been able to stem the tide of devil worshipers.

While innocent persons were being condemned and killed, the true practitioners of evil flourished—underground. They formed covens and secret societies, held meetings, and conjured up evil in all the ways they could possibly conceive of.

The black masses of today, held every night in thousands of gathering places throughout America, started in the Middle Ages as an outcry against Christianity and the Church. Originally, these meetings were a means of symbolic rebellion for the peasants against the powerful, rich Church. The practices were adopted by those who desired power themselves by using the evil force.

The Sabbath is the seventh day of the Hebrew week, a day set aside by the Fourth Commandment for rest and rejoicing. In black-art rituals, the words "black Sabbat" are used to denote the day for feasting and coming together. (There are many words associated with the black arts that are taken from the Hebrew. It is a historical fact that early Christian scribes and priests purposely utilized Jewish or Mohammedan words to describe works of evil. Non-Christian religions were maligned by associating them with devil worship. What better way to describe the evil things that occurred in the black arts and the occult world than to misuse the words of other religions? The word "synagogue" was sometimes used in place of "witches' Sabbath." How devious is man.)

Some black-art historians go so far as to state that early Christian leaders fabricated the ideas of covens and black masses themselves. When they accused someone they wanted to do in, it was much easier to say that another member of the coven afforded them the necessary information. It was also easier to spy on groups that met, rather than on an individual. Until those early Christian inquisitions, it seems that most persons involved in devil worship or the black arts did so alone and were not organized into groups.

From the fourteenth century on, the meetings, masses, and covens grew in number. The main features of the Sabbats or black masses were:

1. The assembly. The unification of those persons involved. The idea of thirteen forming a coven is relatively new, as history states that early black masses were celebrated by groups as large as a hundred or more.

2. Homage to the Devil. Once assembled, the celebrants performed rituals, such as baptisms or marriages in the name of Satan, and—most important—the verbal statement of the advocates' allegiance to the Devil.

3. A banquet, usually of raw foods, purported to be aphrodisiac. Gluttony was also indulged.

4. The festivities. Frenzied, lurid dancing and indiscriminate sexual acts.

There were variations of the above, but in general black masses even now tend to follow the rules.

Once the ideas of the masses and covens were brought to prominence by early Christian leaders, they became more popular than ever and gained more committed—Darker—adherents. Evil forces had used the Christian religious leaders to aggrandize themselves.

During the Age of Enlightenment, the eighteenth-century movement toward rationalism and skepticism, the black arts began to be either denounced or ridiculed. Those who believed in the black arts were thought hopelessly stupid. Yet evil power continued, out of fashion as it was, to thrive.

Only once in America did the pursuit of evil take on the horror that had infected most of Europe. That, of course, was in the Salem witch hunts of 1692. Having had a personal experience concerning Salem (brought to light at the Ouija board), and having done much investigation into the subject, I am convinced that the young maidens of Salem who accused others of witchcraft were indeed utilizing an evil force themselves. Those they accused, however, were probably innocent. The accusers were truly possessed by an evil force, I believe, and their mentor was the evil slave Tituba. This woman, steeped in the ritual and evil conjuring of Africa and the Caribbean, was guilty of unleashing the Devil in the early American colonies. It is too bad that in popular literature she has come to represent innocent stupidity, for she was cunning enough to save her own neck and falsely accuse nine persons, most of whom were put to death.

Thirteen persons were hanged and more than a hundred and fifty imprisoned before the good men of Salem came to their senses. In all probability, there were those in Salem who were guilty of consorting with the Devil, besides the vile youngsters who condemned the innocents. It is also most probable that the true evildoers and followers of Satan completely escaped the fate of the others. Even the evil-seeking Tituba was released.

Devotees of the black arts have come to the fore in numbers at various other times of our country's history. Usually, outbreaks occur before a war or some other impending danger. There are those who seek solace in a universal answer to things; and many do not have the desire, the humility, or the strength it takes to turn to God, or the good forces.

The recent upsurgence in the popularity and dissemination of the black arts may be explained by several factors. The youth of today are generally antiestablishment, and what better way to go against their elders' teachings and beliefs than by turning to the mystical, Satanic religions? Also, many people today see the revival in the occult and black arts as a response to the failure of science and more conservative, God-following religions to make the world a better place in which to live. Indeed, it may sometimes appear that scientific advances have helped to destroy the sanity and love in the world. So why not turn to opposite ways and teachings?

Many religious and government leaders of today make light of the current interest in the Devil and black-art investigation, stating that the interest is at best superficial—that many persons are simply amusing themselves for want of more interesting things to do and learn, now that the mystery has been taken out of everything. And this is exactly what the evil forces would like to have those in charge believe.

Young people are enticed by the offerings of those who would seek to build their own images and spread the evil work at hand. Drugs, sexual indulgence, the freedom to do as one pleases are the main come-ons.

A typical leader of a black-art group is Anton LaVey, often referred to as "the Black Pope," who came to the fore in 1966, when he announced the formation of the Church of Satan. LaVey's "church" utilizes a mixture of the black aspects of the occult, voodoo, the teachings of Aleister Crowley's Satanic circle (which thrived in Victorian and Edwardian England), plus the works of the Black Order of Germany (which reached its peak in that country's decadent nineteen-thirties). The First Church of Satan carries out black-magic deeds in the open instead of underground, as is usually the practice with covens and other black-art groups.

The life LaVey led as a youngster was indeed different and strange. He was a child prodigy, spending most of his time studying music, metaphysics, and the occult. He always hated the hypocrisy of Christian religions and began to question God's role in the world.

He became a magician's assistant and learned how to perform hypnosis when he was still in his teens. By the time he was an adult, Anton LaVey was holding ritualistic black-magic meetings in his home. He used many books about the black masses in his early teachings, works that had evolved from groups such as the Knights Templars (dating back to the early twelfth-century Crusaders) and the Golden Dawn (in nineteenth-century England). His main purpose was "to gather a group of like-minded individuals together for the use of their combined energies in calling up the dark force in nature that is called Satan."

He performed devious rites in the name of the Devil—weddings, funerals, lust rituals to help individuals fulfill their sexual desires, and destruction rituals to assist members of the Church of Satan to triumph over enemies and attain their evil goals in life.

The Church of Satan has a code of precepts called the Nine Satanic Statements. They are as follows:

1. Satan represents indulgence, instead of abstinence.

2. Satan represents vital existence, instead of spiritual dreams.

3. Satan represents undefiled wisdom, instead of hypocritical self-deceit.

4. Satan represents kindness to those who deserve it, instead of love wasted on ingrates.

5. Satan represents vengeance, instead of turning the other cheek.

6. Satan represents responsibility to the responsible, instead of concern for psychic vampires.

7. Satan represents man as just another animal, sometimes better, more often worse than those that walk on all fours, who, because of his "divine spiritual and intellectual development," has become the most vicious animal of all.

8. Satan represents all of the so-called sins as they all lead to physical, mental, or emotional gratification!

9. Satan has been the best friend the Church has ever had, as he has kept it in business all these years.

The Church of Satan adherents follow nineteen mystical keys, which when repeated will bring about their desires. A set language is used in the Satanic rituals—Enochian, which is thought to be older than Sanskrit. It first appeared in print in 1659 in a biography of two well-known seers and astrologers of the sixteenth century, John Dee and Edward Kelley.

Anton LaVey has translated the Enochian keys, and he says, "The meaning of the words, combined with the quality of the words, unite to create a pattern of sound, which can cause great reaction in the atmosphere. The barbaric tonal qualities of this language give it a truly magical effect which cannot be described." After having read these keys carefully, I have decided not to quote them in their entirety in this work. They are of such a powerful nature that even an excerpt might very easily be of assistance in conjuring up the evil forces that would be the only reason for reciting the keys.

The last paragraph of the nineteenth key sums up the previous eighteen. It "commands the gates of Hell to open wide," demanding that the lower heavens beneath serve the subjects' own purposes. It commands those who are reciting the words to "arise and move and appear before the covenant of His [the Devil's] mouth, which He hath sworn unto us in His justice." It demands that the "mysteries of His creation be unfolded to those who follow Satan and that they be able to partake of the UNDEFILED WISDOM."

Voodoo, an extension of the black arts, has been on the rise in the United States. The term *voodoo* specifically refers to the folk religion of Haiti, and derives from the Dahomean (West African) *vodun,* meaning "spirit." The voodoo religion is syncretic—it is composed of African, Roman Catholic, and local elements. As practiced now in Haiti, it is the height of devil worship. Sex plays the most important role in voodoo. Weird rites are performed by those who indulge in this vile form of worship. Women of the cult are debased, they are used merely and specifically as sexual slaves to their men. They are made to perform in a masochistic manner for the males, even on the wedding night.

When I visited Puerto Rico in 1971, I made a side trip to see a *houngan,* the voodoo name for "priest." I had been sought out for a private psychic consultation by a voodoo practitioner who had read about my arrival on the island. In return for the reading, the young black man had asked me if I wished to visit the place of a voodoo priest. Since the young man was a most successful shop owner in the luxurious business area known as Old San Juan, I decided to take him up on his invitation. (Voodoo is not common to Puerto Rico but spread there from Haiti.)

The site for the voodoo *hounfort* (a kind of compound where the houngan lives) I was to visit was high on one of the countless and lovely mountains that cover the interior of Puerto Rico. A narrow path had been macheted out of the lush green wilderness, and it led to the *hounfort.* About halfway up the path, I decided that I was most probably making a mistake. But it was too late to turn around.

We reached the *hounfort* and I was given something to eat and drink. The *houngan* was introduced to me and seemed not too frightening. He was originally from Haiti and was practicing his voodoo without sanction from the Puerto Rican government. I was asked never to betray the location of the *hounfort.* I vowed that I wouldn't.

The *houngan* had a makeshift altar in his dwelling hut. On the altar were pictures of Jesus Christ, the Virgin Mary, and various saints. Dead plants, vinelike things that had withered from neglect, were placed between the pictures. Several empty beer and Coke bottles, a butcher knife, and glasses filled with or half empty of rum were also scattered on the altar.

It was near evening and I was asked if I wished to stay and witness a ceremony. I do think that the *houngan* thought of me as being involved in work similar to his—at least, that is why, I believe, he allowed me to remain. I agreed to stay, but only if no animal sacrifice was to be performed. I was told that this was not to be a sacrificial rite.

Several extremely talented drummers began to beat out fantastic rhythms on variously sized drums. They were seated in the compound directly in front of the *houngan*'s house. About twenty other people were also present. I hadn't noticed them earlier, they just seemed to be there when the drums began their erotic pulsations.

The guests began to dance, simulating copulation. The *houngan* himself commenced to dance among them, acting out grotesque sexual acts with his movements. Several of the dancers spun around in circles until they appeared to be in a trance of sorts. They then yelled out strange utterances, which I was later to learn were of a predictive nature, regarding friends and relatives.

Voodoo practitioners call spirit entities *loa,* who are known by the names of certain Catholic saints and African gods. The participants believe that by dancing themselves into frenzied states the *loa* will come into their bodies and take possession of them, at least during the period of the ritual. They sometimes fall to the ground and writhe in fits, allowing the forces from beyond to possess them.

A woman came into the dancing throng and handed two white chickens and a knife to the *houngan.* I knew that a sacrifice was indeed going to be performed. Quickly, I found the man who brought me to the *hounfort* and asked him to take me out of there. We left.

I was later told that sacrifices are the most important aspect of voodoo rituals, for in many cults blood is needed to appease evil voodoo gods. Usually, a pig or a goat is offered up and slaughtered in the most cruel manner. If the animal is male, its testicles are cut off while it is alive. It is then beaten and tortured before the *houngan* puts an end to it with his knife. Dogs are often used, their tails and ears cut off before death. The chickens I saw brought into the ceremony would have their legs and wings slowly crushed before death eliminated the horrendous pain they experienced.

Voodoo gods are as sexual as they are bloodthirsty. Erzulie, a powerful voodoo goddess, is worshiped in a most peculiar way. Every Thursday and Saturday evening female voodoo followers light countless candles, make beds of clean sheets, and then go outdoors and sleep in the fields, as their husbands make erotic gestures to Erzulie, trying to attract her attention. Masturbation completes the husband's night, as he imagines that he is copulating with Erzulie.

Some voodoo cults are directly involved with Satan. Members of particular sects will sell the soul of a loved one to the Devil if in return he will grant them prosperity for one year. It must be the soul of someone whom they love, such as a mother, mate, or child. After the entire family has been sold to the Devil, one at a time, the desperate voodoo adherent will finally offer his own soul to Satan.

The practices of voodoo, as loathsome as they are, have taken hold in many areas of our country. Voodoo can usually be found in slums and near-slums, as it is in Africa and South America, being in many cases the only activity that breaks the horrible boredom and poverty.

Before I began research for this book, I thought that many people had been helped in some way by probing the unknown. Now, I am convinced that it is quite the opposite, that more souls have been harmed by involving themselves in the occult world. One of the most well-known examples is Aleister Crowley.

Crowley was born in England in 1875. He attended Cambridge, where his investigations into the occult began in earnest, although he had always expressed an interest in psychic matters. While at Cambridge, Crowley became angered with one of the masters there. Having read extensively about black-art rituals and the power contained therein, Crowley attempted to place a curse on the master who had reprimanded him.

One night, when the moon was full, Crowley took a group of gullible followers into the meadows that surrounded Cambridge. Reciting evil incantations, Crowley extracted a waxen image from his coat pocket. The image, he told the group, was that of the master who had slighted him. Crowley then produced a long, sharp needle. The group was frightened. Just as Crowley was about to stick it into the image, one of the youthful followers became frightened and broke out of the ring that he and his companions had been asked to make. He lunged at Crowley's arm, attempting to knock the needle to the ground. The needle slipped and pierced the leg of the waxen image. At that point the group broke and ran, some frightened, others with jokes on their lips.

The following day, the master whom Crowley had tried to curse tripped on the college steps, breaking his ankle.

Crowley had other minor successes with his delvings into black magic. In the late 1800's Crowley became a member of the Order of the Golden Dawn, a black-art group of then more than a hundred members, even though it was most secret. Among its members was MacGregor Mathers. He and Crowley became, possibly out of jealousy, arch enemies. Through maneuvering, Mathers got Crowley thrown out of the order. Crowley then formed his own group devoted to black-art rituals, the Order of the Silver Star. Mathers died a mysterious death in 1918, and his close friends have sworn that Crowley put a death spell on him.

Crowley stayed for a time in Sicily, where he lived with the disciples at the Abbey of Thelema, near Cefalù. Satanism was practiced at the abbey, and animal sacrifices were offered up to the Devil by the men and women who inhabited the place. The Italian government got wind of the weird black-art practices at the Abbey of Thelema, and when it learned that human infants born to the disciples were also being killed in rituals, Crowley was expelled from Italy.

He then went to France. In Paris, so the story goes, he learned what power evil has. Crowley had a son, MacAleister, who was as interested in the strength of evil as his father was. Together, they decided to raise the Devil and use him for their own purposes.

One particular Saturday evening, Crowley, his son, and eleven of their adherents went to a small hotel that belonged to one of Crowley's followers. The owner of the hotel was asked to empty a large room at the top of the stairs of its furniture and trappings. "My son and I are going upstairs to this room," Crowley told the others. "The rest of you will remain here. Whatever sounds or disturbances you may hear, do not come up. You are not to enter the room until dawn." The eleven were given incantations and chants to perform during the time Crowley and his son would be left alone in the room.

Crowley and his son went up to the room and closed the door. And as the night progressed, the remaining eleven heard much noise, shouting and stomping. They heeded Crowley's command, however, and did not go upstairs.

In the morning they went to the door of the room and

knocked. No answer. They banged at the door. Not a sound from within. Finally, out of desperation, they broke down the door.

What they found has become a little-explained fact in occult history. Cowering in one corner of the room was Aleister Crowley, naked, his black-art robes torn from his body. His son lay dead in the center of the room, his face twisted in the most agonized, fearful manner. The medical report was that MacAleister died of fright, the victim of a heart attack.

Aleister Crowley spent the next four months in an insane asylum, reduced to a blithering idiot. When he emerged, he was quite harmless, and remained so for the rest of his life. What was conjured up in the room has not ever been completely explained. Most probably, the force they had encountered was a bit more powerful than even they might have imagined, and for some unknown reason it had turned on them.

Justin Kopley is a young man in his twenties. He is a college graduate with two degrees, one in English, the other in art. But he spent his first year of college—a noted school on the East Coast, one with most stringent entrance requirements—as a psychology major. After two years in school, Justin met Vaughn. This young man was eighteen, a freshman on campus. It was obvious from the start that Vaughn was different, even a bit strange. He continually interfered with other people's business. He liked to mess up relationships, especially those of the heart.

Justin was introduced to Vaughn by a mutual friend, a student named Marie, with whom Justin had been intrigued because of her interest in occult matters. Marie had professed to him that white magic was an art she had read much about and even had dabbled in.

Vaughn told Justin of his keen interest in things pertaining to the subconscious mind and the deeper mysteries. "My grandfather fooled around with the kabala," Vaughn said, "and told me where I could acquire two more volumes. The final books I'll have to find on my own some day. When I do, I'll have all the power necessary to do as I wish."

The kabala is an ancient Hebrew system of theosophy, consisting of various books and quite mystical in nature. Although originally meant for good, to conjure up benign manifestations of God's will, the kabala has been misused since medieval times. Kabalistic lore has been utilized by some seekers of power to summon up evil.

Vaughn became more inclined toward the mystical as his college days progressed. He delved into hypnotism and other mental experiments. Justin has told me that there were not one but two covens on the campus of his school. "One night I came upon a group of hooded students carrying candles and chanting as they milled around one of the crypts on the campus. The feeling I got was quite ominous. I'm sure that Vaughn had a lot to do with those covens being formed then."

Vaughn was not an attractive young man. He was very short and indeed quite ugly. Yet as his college days went on, it was apparent that he attracted girls. When questioned by Justin and other students, the girls would say that they really didn't know why they went out with Vaughn, he simply drew them to him. Some young women became frightened when they discovered themselves in Vaughn's room after midnight, not remembering how they got there. Several female students said that they had awakened in the night, had dressed, gone to Vaughn's room, and spent the night with him. They said that Vaughn acted as though he had been expecting them.

Fascinated by this youth and his seeming power, Justin

and a few other students questioned him, whereupon Vaughn again affirmed his interest in the kabala and other mystical forms. "Come over to my room some night and I'll show you what my experiments into the supernatural have thus far produced," he said.

Justin and another friend took him up on his invitation. When they got to the dormitory, a beautiful Tudor-style building, with carved wooden walls and ceilings, Vaughn greeted them and led them to his room, also Tudor in style, with high ceilings and carved, intricate woodwork.

Vaughn took out his book of the kabala. He sat down for several minutes and told his guests that he was working out the mystical numbers to do the thing he desired to accomplish that evening. He then got up and removed a carpet from the inlaid wooden floor, revealing a pentagram which he had painted.

Standing in the center of the pentagram, Vaughn began to recite numbers, forward then backward. He chanted an incantation. Stripped to his shorts, with no undershirt on, Vaughn clapped his hands together and produced three marijuana cigarettes.

"This is the power I have. I always get what I ask for," Vaughn proudly told his two companions.

At first, Justin attributed the marijuana incident to some kind of magical trick that Vaughn had mastered. But he and the other student had watched him so closely that it seemed impossible for the trick to be done in any physical way.

Sometime later, Justin and Vaughn had a discussion regarding evil. Vaughn made the direct statement, "There are some persons completely devoted to evil."

Justin told Vaughn that there was some good in everyone, that no one could be entirely devoid of good.

"I've totally renounced good for evil," Vaughn proudly said to Justin.

"But some good has to remain, you couldn't be completely evil." Justin could not bring himself to believe that a person would allow himself to be entirely, and knowingly, enveloped in evil.

Vaughn said, "Oh, but I am completely evil. I've made a pact with the Devil. In order to do this, I've had to renounce all good for evil."

Other students were present during this conversation, and one of them asked if Vaughn had ever seen the Devil.

"Yes, I have," Vaughn said.

"Can you summon the Devil at will?" another skeptical but fascinated student inquired.

"Yes," Vaughn replied. "I've done it several times." Most of the group laughed. "You don't believe me? Come, I'll show you," Vaughn beckoned, asking them to come to his room for a demonstration.

Five students, including Justin, went up to Vaughn's room. Once again, Vaughn stood inside the pentagram. This time he recited several different incantations and various numbers. The five students were seated in a circle around the pentagram.

A cloud of black smoke suddenly emanated from the center of the pentagram. Justin and the others were convinced that it was a trick of some kind, effective but something any good magician could achieve. Within an instant, however, their skepticism disappeared. Out of the smoke a huge thing emerged. It slowly began to grow in size until its height was from floor to ceiling.

"It had black wings," Justin told me, "and cloven hooves. Long horns came out of its head, which was that of some wild beast."

"What did you do?" I inquired.

"What did we do? The five of us ran the hell out of that place as fast as possible."

I was really intrigued with what it was that Vaughn

had indeed been able to conjure up and I showed Justin many pictures of the Devil in various black-art books. When we came to a painting of Baphomet, Justin said that it was this which he and the other four students had seen that night in Vaughn's room.

Baphomet is an evil deity worshiped by Arab mystics for centuries. It is said to represent the Absolute in magical form. Its head and hooves are that of a goat. Its hands are human and its thorax and abdomen are covered with fishlike scales. Baphomet is hermaphroditic, having both a vulva and a penis. On its forehead is a pentagram.

It was Baphomet which the Knights Templars were accused of worshiping when their order was suppressed by Philip IV of France and the Pope in the early fourteenth century. The Order of the Knights Templars was formed in 1118, at the time of the Crusades, in order to go to the Holy Land and protect Christian pilgrims who were arriving there in ever-increasing numbers. The order consisted of the best knights from many nations. They soon became corrupted, however, and indulged in every vice. Many of them became rich from spoils, though they had been sworn to poverty. They were first based in Malta, and they dominated and bled the Mediterranean for many generations. In a short period of time, some sources relate, the Order of the Knights Templars forsook Christ and gave themselves over to the complete worship of Baphomet.

The Order of the Knights Templars spread throughout Europe and established headquarters in France. Philip the Fair, the King of France, found himself short of funds and decided to take the treasure of the Knights Templars, which he had heard was amassed in the Temple, the great fortified monastery in Paris. The king made contact with Pope Clement V and enlightened him about the horrendous blasphemies the wicked members of the order were committing. The Pope gave the king permission to strike out against the order.

King Philip invited the Grand Master of the Order, Jacques de Molay, along with various other important Knights Templars to the Louvre, where they were to be royally entertained. The Templars accepted. Upon their arrival at the Louvre, they were arrested. Heresy charges were brought against them, and they were all eventually burned at the stake. King Philip confiscated the treasure of the Order of the Knights Templars for his own use.

Jacques de Molay, who was said to have been very close to the evil forces, put a curse on the royal house of France as the flames leapt about his tortured body. It is most interesting to note that later, when the French monarchy ended with the execution of Louis XVI and his family, the last place the monarchs stayed was the Temple, the previous home of the Knights Templars. They were kept prisoner there until the ride to the guillotine. The curse had taken effect.

Baphomet still figures in various black-magic rituals, especially in the Middle East. Justin and his friends had seen this ancient, evil deity come to life in front of their eyes.

When I asked Justin what had happened to Vaughn since those school days, he said that Vaughn had left college and had gone to London, where he had acquired the second book of the kabala. The last he heard of him was that Vaughn was traveling to Israel and other Mideastern countries seeking the rest of the books that make up the kabala.

There are many things that cause deep concern in this story. That a college of renown had covens on the campus is distressing enough. But that students like Vaughn are seeking to utilize the power of Satan is even more alarming. And why must people like Justin and the other students feel the need to investigate black-art teachings? Is it not the general lack of spiritual involvement today? Is it not the backlash to our immersion in materialism and commercialism?

I met Steve at a Christmas Eve party. He was the fiancé of a close friend. Steve was a psychology major and had just graduated from college when we were introduced. He had expressed a desire to meet me, having read my books in school and maintaining a keen interest in matters of the occult.

We talked for quite a while and soon I became aware that he was deeply concerned about something. I could sense that he wanted to question me but was holding back.

"What's bothering you?" I finally probed.

"Well, to tell you the truth, Daniel," Steve replied, his eyes averted from mine, "I feel that I have incurred karma of great significance in this life and I am truly perturbed by it."

"What is it that you have done?" I inquired.

"Well, when I was in school, there was a group of friends who were interested in the occult, four boys and one girl. We read a lot of books, you know, the kind you can get anywhere, at any bookstore or drugstore counter. Mostly, we were absorbing things about magic—black magic—mixed with science fiction and the like." Steve paused and took a sip of the Christmas punch. His hand shook as he reached for the glass.

"Anyway, there was this particular guy on campus," Steve continued. "No one liked him, he was really gross, and the five of us who were into the black-magic scene talked about him one night. One of us said that we should try some of our magic, occult stuff, on this guy. At first, it was said as a joke, but we began to talk about it seriously. If we did try something magical on him, we would be killing two birds with one stone; we would prove or disprove magical powers, and we would be getting rid of this pain in the neck."

At this point, anticipating the climax, I reached for my own glass of punch. As Steve related the story to me, I began to wonder if students everywhere were not delving into the black arts. This was about the fourth confession in a month that I had had from college students who had been involved in the darker aspects of the psychic.

"We got some books together, some with details on how to do black-magic spells and the like. We drew a pentagram and did the whole scene. It seemed like an elaborate game, and we really got into it. We worked on this guy for a week or two, nightly. The end result of this was that we indeed did get rid of the pain in the neck; he had a complete nervous breakdown and was taken away. He did get well, later, but he never returned to the school."

Steve paused, and then continued, running his words quickly together, almost afraid that he wouldn't get them out if he took too long a time to spell out his confession in all its horror. "We had proven ourselves to be successful at our magic and we decided to meet more often, attempting other spells and rituals, some good, some bad. But after our third or fourth meeting we were, in a strange way, stopped from continuing. After each successive meeting, within several days of our getting together, one of us would break a leg, or an arm. There were three bones broken, all told, and we took this as some kind of sign. We ceased our meetings altogether. I am really quite concerned, as I do feel as though I have incurred karma. Unfortunately, I did not know too much about karma or the true, spiritual side of things before I became a part of the black-art rituals we five got involved in."

My reply to this young man was simple and direct. I told him that I felt that he had incurred karma because of the young man on whom they had performed black magic; that was if indeed they were responsible for his nervous breakdown. What he had described to me led me to believe that they had produced the atmosphere in which the nervous disorder of the young man could fester and grow into a breakdown. Hopefully, by recognizing his actions as a grave mistake, the young man will work this karma out.

The dark, evil forces are gaining strength every day, and the more highly evolved energies are losing ground. As I am writing this, I have received word that a friend of mine decided to investigate the powers of the Devil. When asked why, he replied that one must know the strength of the Devil before it can be conquered. If one is to move toward the Light, he said, one must experience its opposite, evil. And that's like taking poison to prove that you can die from it.

Tuning into the world of psychic phenomena and the occult is dangerous for those who do not understand their basic laws. The occult is not a study to be taken up as a game or an amusement. Those persons who use the occult to entertain and thrill friends or audiences are as much to blame as the others who haphazardly seek them out in order to be thrilled.

When I was involved in Spiritualism, I was upset many times by mediums who indeed were psychic and brought forth evidence that a loved one was present in the room. So often they stop there, only capable of expressing evidence that life continues. It wasn't enough that my Aunt

Anna could be brought into a séance. I always felt that progressive, intelligent, and constructive forces from the other side would not merely come to me just for the excitement of having them appear. I demanded more from the other side—some constructive, informative, or meaningful guidance.

Evil spirits, entities who are earthbound or malicious, are always on the watch for those of us who might permit them to come into our lives, as playthings for an evening's entertainment. These spirits are out to destroy those who would conjure them up.

Sigmund Freud, on his deathbed, said that if he had had his life to live over, he would have been a parapsychologist, as he felt that this was where the truth of most of our problems was held, in the psychic part of our minds.

Until more stringent and scientific attitudes in regard to the world of the occult are taken, I suggest that one should not delve into its depths. Many have gone into black magic and have been harmed in some major way—or have not returned.

CHAPTER 4

THE CHANGE I FELT WITHIN ME WAS CERTAINLY MOST pronounced. I was fully aware of what I was doing. Everything seemed more vibrant, more alive.

Music was ecstasy—I was able to enter into each note, to perceive forthcoming melodies with gleeful anticipation, to glide over and beyond rhapsodic scales, then experience forceful crescendos.

Never had I been more cognizant of such color! Even the muted tones of a gray winter sky appeared to glow with what amounted to a completely new sense of vision.

And food . . . ! My God, what an experience that was! The almost excruciating taste, the fantastic *taste* of things. Every bite of even a piece of plain white bread—like munching on the most succulent morsel of steak you could imagine.

My bearskin rug in the living room next to the fireplace—the feel of it almost unbearable to the touch. The warmth of burning embers brought unyielding comfort, almost a kind of sexual gratification.

Wisps of curling smoke from burning incense floated into receptive nostrils, and breathing deeply, I took in every bit of the odor, like a miner gasping for air after having been trapped in a cave.

My physical senses, titillated and utilized to their utmost capacity, afterward brought upon me a total exhaustion, a state of near-frenzy, of not being able to cope with the world as it was.

I am describing the effect upon *me* the first time I smoked marijuana. It was a test of sorts, and I wrote down everything that occurred that night. Many psychics have recorded effects upon their sixth sense after indulging in various forms of drugs, usually under scientific supervision. I had decided to do it independently in my own home, with friends present.

My initial reaction to the drug was that I seemed to know things automatically, without trying, without tuning in, without meditating or actively working at it. I felt able to enter into my friends' minds and I welcomed them into mine. I would laugh, and the person opposite me would laugh, each realizing the joke in what was about to be stated by one of us—at least, we had the *impression* that we knew each other's thoughts.

Time meant nothing—zero—no minutes, no hours. A half hour could have been a lifetime, an hour passed as if it were merely a second.

Space . . . floating . . . a kind of levitation; a form of astral projection.

And what about my psychic center? After all, that is what the experiment was about.

With honesty I can state that over a period of several months, having taken marijuana on succeeding occasions, I found it didn't at all enhance my psychic awareness. In fact, my psychic ability became dulled as my physical appetites heightened.

That feeling of knowing others' thoughts is just that—an impression. You react and they in turn react, usually to something entirely different from what each of the participants is thinking. Whenever I asked the other person if what I thought he was thinking was correct, he would say no—and vice versa.

Marijuana and alcohol (of which I hardly ever partake) offer nothing more than temporary relaxation, temporary escape from cares, temporary heightened physical sensations. They do this by attacking that part of the mind known as the subconscious—temporarily eliminating the energetic forces which make up that section of the brain and replacing it with a heightened consciousness. Over prolonged use, drugs will destroy the subconscious, replacing it with needs to fulfill only conscious physical desires.

The more potent drugs such as LSD, over a period of time, block the subconscious completely, eventually making monsters of their users. Evil forces have a ball with those advocates and disciples of drug use.

"Coming down" from drugs, including alcohol, is one of the worst physical feelings to experience. To be "hung over" is not worth all the seeming joy that came before. I have described the near-ecstatic feeling that overcame me the first time I used marijuana. I shall also not ever forget the first time the drug wore off.

The music I had "grooved on" still played, but whereas I had become a part of it during my "trip," the now too loud, a bit discordant, and repetitious sound of the latest Blood, Sweat, and Tears record seemed merely annoying. The colors I thought I had sensed in the gray winter sky were now more lifeless than they were before I had smoked. The white bread I had eaten with pleasurable gusto had simply the dull taste of bleached, unappetizing flour.

This is reality brought to its apex. I can see why many of our young people become potheads or addicted to more potent drugs. After I came down from my first drug experience, I found it almost impossible to cope with the real world. Although friends have told me that this experience is an unusual one in the case of marijuana, I did find it difficult to accept material things as they really are. If I did not have more control, I could very easily become addicted to drugs or alcohol, seeking a more powerful "high," seeing things as they might or could be rather than as they are.

Alcohol and drugs make it easy for the Darker elements of the universe to take hold of one's soul. They are a tool of evil, and evil utilizes them like no other force on earth.

I have witnessed the destruction of several members of my family through misuse of alcohol; and within the last few years, I have been able to view the effects of evil on those who use drugs vainly to seek enlightenment, which, no matter how much the physical senses are affected, is not forthcoming.

In 1971 and 1972, I spent much time with young people in Woodstock, New York, a town not far from my home. Many of these people were, and still are, into the drug culture—experiences from a marijuana high to an LSD trip, from opiated hashish to amphetamines.

And do you want to know the sadness of it? The fact is that these people who tell you that the drugs they are taking afford them a liberating freedom, a release from worldly cares, an ability to enter into euphoria, a spiritual state of bliss, are in truth the most unfree, negative-thinking, unhappy, physically and spiritually lacking group of human beings I have ever encountered.

Tragic? More than that—for here are some souls being

lost to the Darker forces through well-disguised elements of evil.

Robert is a young man in his early twenties that I met in Woodstock. He became a friend of mine, and of Eileen Dent's during one of her visits to my home. Robert is into drugs. He told us that he has taken LSD more than a hundred times. Marijuana is a daily habit. Robert is incapable of functioning without drugs of some sort—at least he *believes* that he cannot start the day without drugs. Evil, as stated earlier, does have a way of holding on.

I hasten to add that Robert is a most sensitive, understanding, intelligent person. He is vastly talented both as an actor and a musician. But he has been trapped by a master that has overtaken thousands of other unknowing souls.

You cannot tell Robert anything negative about drugs. He does not listen. I have often received the argument from him, "Listen, Daniel, drugs help me through the day. They give me the courage to face this rotten world, to be myself, to make others happy. They enlighten me. I have gotten to know myself through their use. I can better understand myself and you because of drugs."

Robert truly believes this. Meanwhile, he cannot make a move without them. His talent lies buried in a mass of confused ideologies and misconceptions. He cannot make a decision—one moment he hates certain people, the next moment he says he loves them.

Eileen and I have spent endless hours trying to guide him away from drugs into a better understanding of himself, to make him aware of how he could reach the sublime state of consciousness he seeks through more meditative, spiritual ways. But, alas, the wall is too firmly built.

Robert's habit has now extended to forcing those who enter his home into becoming as stoned as he usually is.

Sentences like "If you really like me, if you want to make me happy, if you wish to share with me, then you will smoke with me" become his weapons against anyone refusing his offer to partake of the drugs he so freely and goodheartedly hands out to all comers.

If Robert spent just half the energy and love in an artistic endeavor as he does in rolling a joint, he could be one of the top talents of his generation. One can only hope that he will see the light—in time. As it is, he indulges more and more each time I see him. There is a point at which you cannot get any more stoned, but Robert tries. He keeps on smoking and pill-popping.

I have seen drugs bring out the Dark, evil nature that lurks in everyone but is usually controlled. We are the sum expression of many lifetimes, and in other lives we have each of us been evil in some way, hence the reason for our return to an earthly existence in the present lifetime.

One of the most dismaying incidents involving drugs happened to an acquaintance of mine. He is one of the top young actors of the day and became a motion-picture star virtually overnight, because of his performance in one of the surprisingly biggest money-making films of the early 'seventies.

And what a human being!—uncomplicated, natural, honest, easy to talk with. Never once did he look down on anyone. He had the most blessed and sought-after gift—the ability to listen, with every ounce of his being. Not only to listen, but to offer his sound advice, which came from an unending source of goodness within.

On the first day that I met him, I turned to his associate, a mutual friend who had introduced us, and said, "My God! This man should have been a psychiatrist, not an actor. His sensitivity and ability to deal with others are beautiful!"

I was truly delighted by his success. But then it happened. Drugs. I was told that he was on LSD and perhaps stronger stuff.

His movies were critically accepted and usually well-received. But his friendships began to suffer, and his appearance changed—bedraggled, wild hair, unkempt, crazed stare—all that the "in" set calls "far out" (and a more apt description was never better applied to a group than those who would copy the hippie-culture uniform as well as its modes of existence just to be "in").

And then came judgment day.

The scene: A crisp spring day in New York City; the initial afternoon's filming of a major motion picture. *The director:* One of the best and most respected of the new men in his field. *The leading lady:* A charming, unaffected, excellent actress.

And the hero: My new acquaintance, whom I had so admired for his qualities of understanding, sensitivity, and warmth.

But on this day, our hero is by now deep into drugs. He has become difficult, moody, and unpredictable. He angers quite easily.

Camera. Action. The director begins the day's work. The actress starts to go through her lines.

"Wrong!" our hero cries. "It's all wrong, you can't act." He tries to take the reins of the film, telling the actress how to emote and the director how to direct. Words fly back and forth. Our hero tells the director off and practically commits assault on the by now horrified actress.

He finally stalks off the set, an action that would eventually result in putting dozens of people out of work and force the film to be canceled.

That evening: Our hero's managers and agents meet with the prospective film's producers and lawyers at his apartment. They all try to calm the freaked-out actor and make him see reason.

Another business associate, just in from the West Coast, is telephoned at his hotel and asked to come over immediately to the meeting. He does so. This famous man has been a close friend of our hero. If anyone can bring the situation into perspective, he is the one—or so everybody thinks.

This man has lost a daughter who took her own life a year previously. She was the love of his life, and the man was almost demolished by the loss. It is the one subject that is not ever mentioned to him by anyone.

As the men discuss the situation, attempting to talk the actor into returning to making the film, the night wears on. There seems to be no headway being made.

The newly arrived man from the West Coast suddenly says, very matter-of-factly as people sometimes do in a situation like this, "If this isn't settled soon, I'm going to kill myself."

The actor turns to him and utters the most dastardly sentence he could. "Just like you drove your daughter into doing?"

Violence. Mayhem breaks loose, the bereft father lunging at our hero's throat. They are separated and the evening ends.

Curtain.

When the story was related to me by people who had been there, I could not believe it. If they had told me the actor had murdered someone, I would have been less surprised. For this usually sensitive, thoughtful man even to think such a thought would have been unlike him. For him to use it as ammunition against a friend staggered the imagination.

His newfound freedom in drugs unleashed in him some ugly, sinister force. He no longer had the protection of control over negative thoughts that might invade his brain.

On another occasion, he came to the office of the man who had introduced us and drew a revolver on the secretary when she said that her boss was not in. This poor soul, this fine artist and basically good person! What a horrible waste. I am told that he is on the road to recovery now, for which I am thankful, as the world should not be deprived of his talent and his true character.

Ron, Louis, and John are three young men I befriended at different times in 1972. They do not know each other. They do have much in common. Each of them has "dropped acid" more than a hundred times. Louis and John have indulged in this by now common LSD practice on at least four hundred separate occasions. When I met them, they had not taken the drug for more than two years, for one of them, four years.

The three young men have all gone to college, where they first learned about drugs. As John says, "If you didn't drop acid you were laughed at as being square, told that you were a jerk, and generally made fun of. I did it to follow the bunch."

The similarities that I have found among these three LSD users are amazing, especially since they come from different places (Alaska, Alabama, and Massachusetts) and different family backgrounds. I have detected a "syndrome" common to these LSD users, and it seems characteristic of far many more users than they.

First, each of these young men has given up on life. They have an "I don't care" attitude. They are quite selfish, critical of the world, but never willing to take a step to change it. They are defeatist in most of their attempts to strive forward. Ron, Louis, and John were extremely creative in their college days. The creative force in them is now dormant. I've heard them belittle and demean themselves physically, mentally, and spiritually. Rarely do they make decisions without agonizing, suffering true horror when confronted with even the possibility of having to make a choice. Once the choice is made, they always regret not having made another one.

The three live on nerves. They are entirely unsettled, forever on the run. They will do anything in order to avoid thinking about themselves and their problems. Each of them loves music. Ron likes acid rock. Louis grooves on old-time, nineteen-thirties and 'forties music. John is into the classics. But each is narrow in his tastes; he resents having to listen to any music other than his favorite kind. The music itself has to be played morning, noon, and night. If Ron goes from the stereo in the living room to his car, where there is a tape deck, he carries a radio for the interim trip. In the many months that I knew him, there wasn't a single time that one of these three instruments was not on.

They cannot sit still for any period of time. There is constant bodily movement. They are defensive and moody —the slightest remark, one not even related to them personally, may set them off.

Their eating habits are strange, to say the least. They are forever noshing on snacks and become disquieted when confronted with an honest-to-goodness complete meal. They never eat at usual hours, but at five in the morning, perhaps, or midnight. They each have a favorite food, one they could spend the rest of their lives eating to the exclusion of all others.

They all have overt idiosyncrasies. John can get into his car at any hour of the night and ride until he is calm or, more likely, exhausted. Louis has a sexual escape, making conquests of anyone who comes into his vibration, with no discrimination at all. Ron occasionally crouches into a fetal position, anywhere, indoors or out, and stays like that for hours on end.

I have tried to introduce them to meditation and spiritual awareness. In each case they said that they couldn't, that they had no patience, and that it would be a waste of time.

Each of them has told me that he had experienced something spiritual when he took LSD. He said he was aware of a force of some kind, but that he either couldn't explain what it was, or was frightened by it.

The three of them find it difficult to express love. They seem confused as to what love is. They have told me that acid made them more aware of their fellowman and that avenues of love were opened up to them, yet none of these three men is able to love. None of them can maintain a relationship for more than a month or so. They expect everything from the one they love, and selfish demands destroy any bond that may develop. Tragically, they are not in the least aware of this selfishness.

These three young men, each one in his way talented and intelligent, have been destroyed by opening up their psychic centers to the living death that comes with drugs. It was apparent to me that the evil forces entered into the minds of these young men while they were drugged and overtook them. Without protection and awareness, they allowed the lower, evil entities to grasp their minds and souls.

Taking acid is like going into a trance immediately after asking beforehand that the most evil forces available enter into one's vibration. Good vibrations are destroyed by drugs, and evil ones are able to fester and multiply in the drug user's mind, until, as in the case of Charles Manson, ultimate control can take place.

* * *

I do not make any moral judgment about drugs; rather a deep-rooted psychic feeling tells me that they open up avenues that can be most dangerous for the user. Spiritual protection can be lost, and the door left ajar for the forces of evil to enter. I do know that there are many persons who use drugs who are not affected, at least not on the surface. They are quite fortunate, for they can control their minds.

I am not speaking as a scientist, a moralist, or an outsider. From my own experiences and those of people close to me, I have seen that drugs can indeed enhance physical experiences, that they do afford temporary freedom from care and give a kind of confidence. But none of these feelings is lasting. In a drugged state, one's consciousness level is bent and toyed with. But the only way truly to reach the inner self, the subconscious, is through meditation, through the development of psychic and spiritual abilities.

The effects of drugs and alcohol eventually wear off. The effects of meditation and spiritual enlightenment are permanent.

Dr. James D. Lisle is a psychologist who is also director of the Helpine Youth Counseling Center in Norwalk, California. In several published statements, Dr. Lisle has stated that it is his opinion that occult practices can develop a hold on some persons in the same manner as drug addiction. His opinions are based upon the associations he has made at the Center with young people who have involved themselves in areas of witchcraft, Satanism, and other devious occult practices.

"You never can be sure that a person involved in this won't step over the line into infant sacrifice or even cannibalism," Dr. Lisle recently said to the press. "We have much evidence that it happens. The people who get involved in a thing like witchcraft have a developing tunnel vision about the world and life. It is a continually narrowing thing that cuts them off from what is going on around them.

"Significant numbers of young people," Dr. Lisle continued, "are substituting the occult scene for the drug scene, or in other instances are combining the two."

Dr. Lisle further has stated that he has discovered very strong psychological parallels between factors that will draw a person into Satanism and the Darker elements of the occult world, and the factors that influence a person to move from occasional marijuana usage to hard-drug addiction.

"In either instance, the drug addict or the person involved in some form of devil worship is very likely to be suffering from powerlessness and seeking power of some kind or he is seeking to gain control over his own life, or in many instances, over the lives of others. He may also be seeking to escape some reality problems in life."

This state of powerlessness may very well be the reason that so many in our society have become involved in devious black-art practices and the more malevolent aspects of the occult. There is an endless accounting of persons who are using the forces of evil for power over others, or using the occult *as* a drug—to escape into a world that is on another level of experience.

CHAPTER 5

CHRISTMAS EVE . . . 1971.

I had decided to spend the day alone. Having completed a move to the new apartment on the West Side, and having only a few days before the end of a tiring lecture tour, I was exhausted mentally as well as physically. I had no desire to host or be hosted by family or friends.

My only companions on that Christmas Eve were my pets, Mia II and Yuki. It was nearing midnight, and the melancholy loneliness which befalls many persons on holidays (especially those without families) unexpectedly struck me full force. I switched on the radio and then the TV, hoping to distract my thoughts from the odd mood that was overtaking me. But the televised Christmas Eve masses only depressed me more. I think it is no coincidence that the largest number of suicides occur during holiday seasons—particularly among those who must spend their days without human companionship.

"Come on, Yuki!" I shouted, leaping from the sofa where I had been sitting. "Let's go for a walk before I begin to enjoy this self-pity."

I put on his collar and leash and bundled up in my winter garments, and then we both went out to breach a cold, clear winter night.

We were on the sidewalk leading into the park, the exact area where I had discovered Mia II. The time was about fifteen minutes to twelve. Not a soul was in sight for blocks, the emptiest I had ever seen a New York street.

There was a three-quarter moon and the night was smogless, giving a rare view of the magnificent Palisades on the opposite side of the Hudson in New Jersey.

Suddenly Yuki came to an abrupt halt. Pointing his wolflike snout up into the air, he began to sniff. He then turned completely around, the hackles on the nape of his neck standing straight up. He let out a howl so filled with terror that the mere recalling of it to this day chills me to the marrow.

I reeled around, expecting to see at least a slew of muggers, guns and knives drawn, converging upon the two of us. Instead, about fifty feet behind, a single man strolled leisurely.

I took Yuki off the path, permitting the man to pass. Yuki never took his eyes off the stranger, who was fairly tall, dressed in gray pants, a black, short coat, and a knitted woolen cap. Under his right arm he carried a black book, which did not strike me as odd, at least then.

The man kept going, crossing under one of the viaducts that carry the West Side Highway; the path he was on led to the Hudson River's edge.

This was the direction in which I was headed. The yacht basin was a short distance away, and I wanted to see the boats with their Christmas lights and decorations.

Passing beneath the viaduct, Yuki again stopped,

sniffed, and howled. This time, he stared and growled toward the stone abutment that holds up the viaduct.

Then I saw him. The stranger. He was propped up against the wall. His eyes were closed, and I could see this clearly because of the lighting system which had been recently installed throughout the park area. The book he had been carrying was now open and he was murmuring. His ashen-white face was composed and relaxed, and he appeared to be in either deep contemplation or some form of meditation.

I continued on my way, took a quick look at the yachts moored in the basin, and then started back. The man was still there, in the same position.

I almost had to pull Yuki to pass in front of the man, who was oblivious to everything. The dog was more upset than I had ever seen him.

As we were about to pass once again beneath the viaduct, I heard a tremendous crash from the highway above. A second, third, and fourth crash took place in succession. I turned back just in time to see the man close his book, smile, and begin to walk away.

I raced up the hill that leads to the highway and found that a four-car chain-reaction accident had occurred.

As I asked the victims of the crash if they needed help, it dawned on me. The man with the black book, open, chanting. Yuki's hysterical reaction to him. His smile and closing of the book at the instant of the crash. Was there some connection? The hill I was on commanded a view of the entire park area. The man was nowhere in sight. I went back down the hill and retraced my steps, but the man was gone.

The incident bothered me for days. I decided that the man and the ensuing accident were coincidences. I certainly did not wish to think that anyone would purposefully do meditative work to create a catastrophe. But I could not shake off the feeling that the man's vibrations had given to both me and Yuki.

Several days later, I went to the Fifth Avenue branch of the New York Public Library. I searched through the books on witchcraft and black magic, volumes which would take months even to scan. After hours of this research, I came upon a book that told of a strange ritual utilized by some devotees of black magic. It said that members of certain black-art groups go out on Christmas Eve, doing evil work, hoping thereby to weaken the powers of good which are celebrated by those who follow the teachings of the master, Jesus Christ. By creating mayhem, these Satan-influenced persons try to do away with the good vibrations that prevail at Christmas.

I firmly believe that the man I saw in the park was a follower of some sort of evil. That he was able to conjure up the accident indicates the power of the Darker elements. Of course, he may have had assistance from the careless driving that goes on during the holiday season. But for the accident to occur directly above his head and then for him gleefully to smile and walk away suggest to me that he was there to accomplish the task.

I did not see this man again, at least for three or four weeks. Then one day, while walking Yuki in the park once more, I came upon him. He was talking with a girl who was wearing a long black-hooded cape. I skirted them.

A week later I saw this girl again. This time she was alone. I approached her, for she was carrying pamphlets and books and apparently selling them. I said a prayer of protection and then began to talk with her.

"Hello." She gave me a big smile. She was young and very pretty.

"Hi, what are you selling?"

"Well, I'm a member of the Process—" She commenced to give me the spiel, but I cut her off before she could continue.

"Yes. I've heard quite a bit about you people."

"Where?" she said, on the defensive. "In that book written about Charles Manson, *The Family*?"

"There, and other places."

"You really don't believe that? It's so untrue, so unfair. It's all a lie."

"Well, I'm in a hurry. May I buy one of your pamphlets?"

"Yes, they're a dollar and seventy-five cents, but I would like to tell you more about us—"

"Well," I said, "let me read the pamphlet first. If it interests me I can always get further information."

I gave her the money and quickly walked away.

The pamphlet is entitled, "The PROCESS . . . On Death." It is actually a magazine, elaborately produced, with the most impressive color drawings, sketches, paintings, and photographs I have seen in a long time. I must add that I found it one of the most dangerous, subversively evil pieces of work I have ever come across. Beneath its lovely pictures and the ideals that speak of the hereafter, there is an underlying—in some instances an overlying—theory that Satan is death and he awaits us, and that we should work to accept him as others have accepted God.

Here are but a few quotes from this evilly wrought magazine:

> *Satan is Death, the separation of soul from body, body from soul. Satan lives in death. My friend, Death is your ultimate test. Satan is the ultimate test of man. In Death, Time ceases to exist. For Satan, Time does not exist; for Satan, there is no past, no future. If we do not accept Death, we cannot accept Life. If we do*

not accept Satan, we cannot accept Christ. Death is Satan's realm; when we go through Death we go through Satan's realm. We cannot run and hide from Satan. Mark you well, all things come to Death in the end.

Cunningly deceiving? Yes, indeed, read it again!

Another quote, this one carefully aligning Jehovah with Lucifer and Satan to make a triumvirate:

> *The three great Gods of the Universe are distinct and separate. They are powerful and they transcend humanity, but they are not limitless. They are definable. The three Gods of the Universe—The Lord Jehovah, the Lord Lucifer, and the Lord Satan. If Jehovah, Lucifer and Satan are brought together, united in a common understanding, a common knowledge, a common bond of awareness and unconflicted intention, then the concept of God becomes a reality. The parts come together to complement each other and make a whole, and the whole is Totality. So, God is the reuniting of the Gods, so that all may become one, having one nature, one substance, one being, one orientation, one power, one truth, one knowledge, one awareness, and having no location either in space or time but transcending altogether the very concept of dimension, then we can say not: God was, God is now and God shall be, but simply, God is.*

If there is one thing I know from my scant religious background, it is that God is not Satan or Lucifer, no matter how fancifully worded the message.

In its section devoted to children, "The PROCESS" has stated a number of guidelines, one of which is "Where possible, avoid any doctrine of virtues or morally superior qualities. Allow children to discover whatever makes them feel good."

I need not go on. Many of the articles and set pieces in the magazine almost refute the forces that motivate this group; but if one reads closely enough, carefully enough, one can find the truth of the nature of the Process.

Eileen Dent was quite upset that I had decided to write this book. She warned me that the forces of evil would try to do all they could to prevent its seeing the light of day, and with thousands upon thousands of advocates, they had quite a power.

"But, Eileen," I protested, "they don't know that I am writing this. No one knows. And besides, the powers of good know that this book is meant to enlighten those who are seeking truth and to help prevent souls from turning themselves over to the powers of evil."

Eileen said, "When those involved in evil sit in meditation, or in gatherings at rituals, they send out their thoughts, forces, vibrations into the ether, to protect themselves from harm, which in their case would be the forces of good. This is the very thing you teach in your classes, which you yourself told me in other words. Daniel, you know the old saying, 'Physician, heal thyself. . . .' "

On many occasions, when sitting down to write this book, I have indeed meditated and said prayers of protection. But as I was at work on the preceding chapter, I left myself momentarily unguarded and the consequences were almost dire.

It was in the dead of winter, and I knew that I could finish quite a bit of writing, secluded in my country home, with the least possibility of interruption.

On the day of my arrival, there was a terrific snowstorm, the worst of the season. Huge drifts made it impossible for me even to leave the house for two days. On the third day, the sun shone brightly, even though the mountain winds blew the snow into blinding, miniature tornados. Most of the time during the first two days was spent digging myself out of the snow and making sure that fuel and fireplace logs were handy, as most electric power in the area had failed.

I was able to accomplish only a bit of writing. My mind was so occupied by the essentials of combating the storm that I did not take time either to meditate or offer myself some other kind of protection.

My food and other necessities were low, and there were warnings of another snowstorm brewing on the horizon. I decided to take the car, ride into town, and equip myself with the necessary rations.

I started out. The car was in fine shape, the motor had warmed immediately. The sun was so strong that I had to put on sunglasses. The winds were now only occasionally gusts. I came to a bend in the road that leads over a built-up section (an abutment) of the reservoir that follows the route into town from my house.

As I turned into the bend, the sun was still shining brightly. Then, within an instant, the entire atmosphere changed. A tremendous gust of wind that did not cease started to engulf both the road and my car. I could not go back or turn around, as the single lane that had been plowed here was now practically covered over with drifts and the rearview mirror showed exactly the same scene that was facing me—a cascading, whirling, turbulent mass of snow.

If I get stuck here, I thought, it could be a disaster. I decided to go on, slowing the vehicle to twenty-five miles per hour. I could see for only three feet in front of the car.

From out of the raging snow in front of me there came without warning a small white car which had been completely camouflaged in the unexpected windstorm. I tried to steer away from the Volkswagen, but it struck my car almost head on. Later I found that the wind had helped to carry it along much faster than the young girl was driving. Her car was sheared almost in half.

Miraculously, neither of us was hurt. But both cars were badly damaged. Only seconds before the crash, I had realized that the storm was very strange, almost unnatural. The sky had become dark and I couldn't see in front of me. I had just begun to say a prayer of protection when the Volkswagen had plowed into my car. My car was still running after the collision, and I got the girl into it and drove away. About sixty feet from the accident, the air was calm, the sun shone as bright as an August day, and there was not a flake of snow.

After exchanging all the information necessary when one is involved in an accident, I drove the girl to her house, then headed back to my own home. After I parked, I sat for about ten minutes, filled with gratitude that no one had been injured. Although my hasty prayer of protection had not prevented the accident, I feel it was responsible for our personal safety. At the end of my meditation, a vision of the man who had upset my Christmas Eve came into my head. And he was laughing.

The accident on that Christmas Eve occurred on a West Side Highway viaduct. The accident I had just had took place on a viaduct that was built up around the reservoir.

I would not sit down again to the task of writing this book without first making sure that every possible form of *protection was afforded me.*

CHAPTER 6

I HAVE MENTIONED A "PRAYER OF PROTECTION" SEVERAL times. This is a prayer which offers a defense against the forces that would seek to harm us psychically or spiritually. It may be some simple words, the Lord's Prayer, a mystical chant, or a lengthy metaphysical reaffirmation of goodness. But whatever form it takes, it works. Without protection, investigation into the occult can be disastrous.

Take the example of Doris Adley, a friend of mine, a thirty-eight-year-old, attractive woman. She lived in a lovely Manhattan apartment, held an excellent high-salaried position, had one child, and was haunted.

From our initial meeting, I sensed an evil vibration around Doris. A mutual friend, Kelly, had introduced us, and at first I thought that Doris merely had bad vibrations. She didn't take to me either.

On my first visit to Doris's charming duplex apartment, I had to excuse myself within an hour of my arrival. For some unexplainable reason, a terrifying fear came over me. It was almost paralyzing. Unable to understand the situation, I felt paranoid—I had to get out, otherwise I felt I would be smothered or in some way harmed by whatever it was that I sensed in the apartment. Afterward, I could offer no reasonable explanation for my odd behavior.

Doris had a son, Alan. He was about thirteen years old, a bit spoiled, somewhat precocious, and very unlikable. I was also unable to put my finger on the reason why I seemed to dislike Alan from the outset.

The second time I went to Doris's was for a birthday party she was giving in honor of our friend Kelly. The proceedings were quite festive, with close to fifty persons present—wine, food, and music filled the gaily lit rooms. But even in this convivial atmosphere, an unyielding sense of melancholy and doom prevailed.

After the party I decided that I would not see Doris again. The fear I felt was impossible to shake, and it was most disquieting, to say the least, either to be in her presence or to visit her home.

When I tried to concentrate psychically on why I felt the way I did around Doris, I was prevented from doing so. My mind drew a complete blank. Even in meditation, all I received was the impression to stay away—far away.

Several weeks passed before Kelly showed me a set of photographs she had taken, of various places at different times. "Daniel," Kelly said, "I just got these back and I can't understand why some of them came out the way they did. You're a good photographer. Can you tell me what went wrong?"

The photographs in question were all excellent and perfectly clear, except for about ten that had been taken at the Adley apartment. I glanced through them and began to experience the same feelings of dread I had received whenever I had been there.

The ten photographs were not blurred or out of focus. They had been taken indoors, but so had the other pictures on the roll. What was wrong with them was that strange lights and flashes seemed to be crossing and crisscrossing over them. The widest and strongest band of light in most of the photos was wrapped around Alan. A fuzzy, tentaclelike light embraced Alan in all of the pictures in which he appeared. You could see the light ray coiled around his small body, like the arm of a giant octopus.

There were no technical errors either in the taking or developing of these photos. They were marked by something in the room other than what was materially there. Anyone seeing them had the same impression of fright that I had when holding them.

A large, glass sliding door opened onto a patio in the Adley apartment. In one of the photos, a face and body clearly could be seen glaring into the room. No one was outside the apartment the night the picture was taken; and even if there had been, I doubt if anyone on earth looks as gruesome and horrifying as that face which was staring point-blank into the camera. Almost prehistoric, devil-like, the face is unforgettable to anyone who sees the photograph.

One day a few weeks later, I was having dinner at Kelly's apartment. Her twenty-one-year-old daughter, Cassey, was also present. We were drinking wine and talking when a vision began to appear in my mind. I rarely have visions, psychic or otherwise; this is not the way my psychic ability expresses itself. The vision was clear, as though a motion-picture screen had been placed in front of my eyes. My eyes were closed but it was as if they were open.

Suddenly Cassey let out a shout. "My God, what am I seeing?"

"What is it?" I asked, at this point petrified.

"It's Doris. I can see Doris's apartment. And . . . it's horrible . . . terrible . . ."

"I'm seeing something too, it's ghastly."

Kelly, completely perplexed, got up from her chair and came over to Cassey and me, who were on the sofa. "What's going on?"

Cassey and I related the common vision we were having. It is the first time I have ever heard of someone having a vision at the same time that another person was experiencing the identical thing.

"I see Doris's apartment," Cassey said.

"So do I," I exclaimed.

"God, do you see the walls? The walls," she repeated.

"Yes." I was shouting by this time. "You mean the blood. All the blood on the walls."

Kelly recoiled in terror. "What the hell is going on?"

"No . . . I don't want to see it. But it's there. Alan, he's hanging over the banister. He . . . he's . . ." The thing was so bad that I couldn't say it aloud.

"He's dead," Cassey completed my hideous thought. "And the blood is pouring from him. Daniel, do you see the downstairs bedroom? The bed?"

"Yes," I said, for I saw it. "It's Doris. Oh, no! How horrible! Who would have butchered them like that?"

At this moment, the vision started to dim. As quickly as it had come to us both, it was leaving. Cassey said that she had the impression that the child had been murdered first, and that Doris had been made to watch.

Kelly was not going to let it go like that. "If you could see that, then it must be a warning of some kind, something that is going to take place. Daniel, Cassey, please try and concentrate and see more. Who else was there? Is there something else?"

Cassey suddenly came out of the trancelike state in which we had both been. I was still not quite out of mine.

completely trust your partner? Can you trust him with the store and all that lies therein? Questions of this nature would appear on her notepaper during many of her automatic-writing sessions. In the beginning, Miss Holly ignored them, preferring to believe they were meant as affirmations of how much she trusted Jim Dawson.

Jim is one of the most honest persons I have ever known. He may have had many problems, but dishonesty was not one of them. He would not take anything that did not belong to him. In fact, he went overboard in the opposite direction. Even if he found something in the street, Jim would not rest until its owner was located. He believed in retribution—that stealing would be dealt with severely; a belief not dissimilar from the base karmic principle that whatever one sows, one reaps.

More and more of Miss Holly's automatic writing warned her of Jim Dawson's dishonesty. At the same time, the entity that worked through her hand began to turn her from contacting me or any other psychic. *Your answers are coming directly from the spirit side*, the entity would write. *There is no need to utilize any other form of psychic advice, you are involved in the highest, most pure form of contacting the forces beyond, there is no need for a medium, YOU are the medium.*

Miss Holly listened to the words of the entity. She became almost cloistered in her room, taking down reams of writing. This aloofness began to worry her friends, for in the past Miss Holly had been a most outgoing, socializing person, one whose days were filled with acquaintances. Jim Dawson attributed this new, unreachable, remote attitude of hers to the pressures of forming and carrying on the new business.

Miss Holly, one day, decided that she needed a vacation. She packed her bags and left, leaving Jim in charge of the store, her apartment, and that which she held most dear, her pet cat. The automatic writing, unfortunately, was continued during her time away from home.

Jim is taking things from you, her pencil would write. *He has backed up a small truck and has stolen many of the new things you have imported from Mexico before they were even taken out of their boxes. He is in the midst of this right now.*

This evil entity now began to write obscenities about Jim, that he was utilizing her apartment for meetings with wanton women. *Jim is bringing various women to your apartment and is using it for sexual activity. There is talk in the entire house about you and your apartment. That which goes on there is indescribable—the drinking, the sex, the depravity.*

Confused beyond sensible thought, Miss Holly rushed home and confronted Jim with his supposed behavior.

"You've used my apartment for your filth and you've stolen so much that is valuable to me," she said harshly.

"Your accusations are insane," Jim protested. "Where have you gotten this insidious information?"

"From the one source that is all-knowing, all-seeing. The entity that writes through my pencil cannot be deceived, and you are guilty and must be punished for this evil activity."

Jim didn't allow Miss Holly to fire him; he quit on the spot. Within a few hours he called and told me the entire story. "What shall I do?" he asked. "Cynthia has gone completely mad. This force has her locked in its embrace and won't let go. She is losing every one of her friends."

I finally managed to contact Miss Holly, whose voice seemed distant and strange. She was not the person I had known and loved in the past. She seemed bent on accusing everyone around her; the force was protecting her, she would say. "Daniel, how grateful I am to have this direct contact with the divine force. It has helped me and guided me. Without its assistance I would have been robbed, cheated, and even done in by those who pretend to be my friends, and who are indeed only out to take those things I have worked for, physically and spiritually."

It was impossible for me to reach her, to explain that what she might have really conjured up was an evil force, which was out to destroy her. Miss Holly would have none of that. After the phone conversation, I was unable to contact her again.

The evil that was brought to life by the automatic writing continued its work. Miss Holly hired a new manager for the store, and he, too, was not safe from the wrath of the wicked thing that wrote the destructive untruths.

Those in the store and in the neighborhood began to see less and less of Cynthia Holly, who now spent all her time with her automatic writing. Finally, the entity got completely out of hand. "Why," she asked aloud, "why am I in this position? Why are all my friends evil? What is causing this evil to come into my life?"

True to form, the force moved her pencil to answer her frantic questioning. *The most evil thing that has brought all of your problems into being is your cat,* the pencil wrote.

"My cat? I love my cat, more than anything in the entire world. She could not be evil."

But she is, the words came, one after another. *She is possessed by an evil spirit and has brought you this bad luck. Watch her. The way she preens herself, the way she sneaks around, stealthy, with menacing eyes. The spirit within her is most evil.*

Miss Holly burst into hysterical tears. Her cat was the only friend she had left and she loved it so. How could it be a channel of evil? But carefully observing the animal,

Miss Holly, in the half-insane world in which she now lived, began to understand the entity's words. The cat did indeed appear to be possessed by a bad force. It crept around on the tables and chairs, apparently lurking near Miss Holly, stalking her. Its eyes told of the evil that was possessing it. The more she watched the cat, the more convinced she was that the words from the automatic writing were correct.

"I've lost all my friends, the business at the store is going down daily, I'm so unhappy, what can I do to change this, to bring about goodness in my life?" Miss Holly's questions were frantic.

In order to bring about complete goodness in your life, the pencil wrote, *you must get rid of that which is bringing the evil into your life. You must get rid of the cat.*

By this time Miss Holly had gone beyond the thin line that separates rational behavior from insanity. She could think only of getting rid of the evil in her life, no matter the cost. "What must I do?" she asked, with a resolution to abide by even the most farfetched words that might come from the pencil.

You must kill the cat tonight. The time is now. The entity knew that it had complete possession of its subject's mind. *Go down into the lobby, into the streets, find an axe, and kill the evil thing.*

Hypnotized by the words that her own hand had written, Miss Holly leapt up, grabbed the cat by the scruff of the neck, and rushed out into the hall. She took the elevator downstairs into the lobby of the elite apartment house and confronted the doorman.

"I must get an axe," she said. "I must rid myself once and for all of this evil that is within my cat. Please, get an axe for me. This cat must die tonight."

The doorman, realizing that he was confronting someone in the throes of a mental breakdown, comforted her and bade her sit in the lobby while he would do his best to fulfill her request. Then the doorman went to the telephone and called Miss Holly's nephew, a frequent visitor to the building.

Within moments the nephew arrived. After a brief struggle, they took the cat from Miss Holly, who by then had gone into deep hysteria. She was taken to the hospital in a taxi. After an examination, the doctors in charge decided that the breakdown was complete and that Miss Holly needed extensive treatment. She was transferred to the mental ward.

Miss Holly underwent months of therapy. She had gone to the point of no return, and electrical shock therapy was prescribed for her in the hope that this painful method of treatment would bring her back. When she was finally released, her mind had come back, but the electrical shock treatments had induced a kind of indifference. The Devil had been shocked from her subconscious, but Miss Holly would never be the person she had been before. The cheerful energy that had characterized her all her life was not evident, and has not yet returned to her.

The evil entity that took complete control of Cynthia Holly did its devious work well. It brought vast, uncompromising horror to her and to those around her. Miss Holly had delved into the world of the occult, unprotected, vulnerable to those forces that are ready to enter the minds and possess the souls of those who are unaware of their power.

CHAPTER 7

There are many occurrences that involve spirits, entities, or what many people commonly call "ghosts." I do not ever refer to spirit forces as ghosts, because this term connotes specifically unpleasant beings—pale things that inhabit old, decaying houses and do harm to those who come in contact with them. At least, that is how ghosts are portrayed in our literature, television, and motion pictures.

I believe that spirits, or ghosts, are the souls of persons who have passed on and for various reasons either remain earthbound or are able to come back to the earth at certain times. Also, it makes sense to realize that an entity, a ghost, continues as it was on earth, in personality and awareness. Therefore there are both good and bad spirits, and many that are in between.

Thus far, I have considered mainly that which is evil, the ghost or spirit who does harm in the world. But there are just as many examples of spirits who come back and do good deeds. Many stories of ghosts tell how they help rather than harm those they "haunt."

In 1943, Parleigh J. Cooper, presently a successful novelist, was seven years old. His childhood until that time had not been one that could be described as joyous. Having lived with various relatives, Parleigh became an introverted, deep-thinking, and lonely boy.

It was in his seventh year, while residing with relatives in Oregon, that young Parleigh first discovered the supernatural force that was to be with him from that time on, a force that would change his life. From the beginning, this force frightened him. Terrified him.

One cold winter's night, the child became aware of a presence in the room. He had been abruptly awakened from a sound sleep, and when he sat up in bed, his fears were confirmed. There, in the doorway to his room, stood a man. Because of fears instilled in him from earliest childhood, Parleigh believed that the Devil had come to pay him a visit. He threw the cover up over his head and tried to shield himself from the evil which he was sure would consume him. He remained wide-awake until morning.

Parleigh was visited by the "thing" on many succeeding occasions. Frightened beyond comprehension, the lad told his family about the stranger who had made himself evident. Parleigh always described the spirit as a person. The family, naturally, felt it was merely childish imagination and let the child know that.

Parleigh's growing fear, however, was very real. The entity would appear at almost any given time or place. Parleigh took to hiding from him. His family would find him crouched in fear behind the stove, under beds, beneath stairwells and other places of refuge.

The spirit was quite definite in appearance to Parleigh,

a man in his midforties. His features were dark, quite Spanish-looking. He wore a long black cape and a strange large hat. The brim of the hat came down partially over the man's brow, casting a shadow which fell just below the eyes. A scarf completed his apparel. The man was about six feet tall.

After a time, the entity began to speak to Parleigh. His speech was at first limited, slow. Eventually, the spirit assured Parleigh that it was not for evil purposes that he had shown himself. He indicated to Parleigh that their meeting had been prearranged, that he was there to help him.

And his appearances enlightened Parleigh. "The being," Parleigh told me, "would place impressions in my mind. I would relate them to my family, and only when the things began to occur did they take heed of this psychic awareness."

The supernatural person never identified himself and Parleigh never asked his name. He referred to him simply as "my man." Parleigh would say, "My man was here last night," or "My man is in the room."

It was Parleigh's man who early on gave him the incentive to become a writer—he became almost possessed with writing and reading. (Today Parleigh feels that his man was a writer in a previous lifetime.)

In his late teens, Parleigh was living in San Francisco. One day his mother, who had divorced and remarried, telephoned him in hysterics. As it happened, Parleigh had been visited by the spirit a few moments before the phone call. His mother could not control her hysteria or bring herself to tell Parleigh what had occurred.

"My stepfather just drove off a cliff and was killed," Parleigh said into the phone, having received that psychic impression during the spirit's visit. That vision proved to be correct, and that was why Parleigh's mother had telephoned.

As Parleigh recently explained to me, "My man always seems to be present when I am down, either spiritually or mentally. If there is a need, my man makes himself evident." Parleigh relates this in a matter-of-fact way. There is no mystery or far-out weirdness about his man. He is simply a fact, as Parleigh sees it.

One evening, when he was returning to his apartment after visiting friends, a car drove by and flashed a spotlight on him. Thinking it some kind of police inspection, Parleigh stood in his tracks as the auto passed him and made a U-turn. As the car started back toward him, Parleigh's man appeared and almost shouted, "Run . . . run quickly!" Parleigh made a dash as the car sped up and tried to catch him. Forewarned, he had a head start and was able to escape by turning several corners.

The following day's newspapers were filled with reports that a hit-and-run maniac had been on the loose the previous evening. After striking his victims, the demented driver threw acid on their faces. The incidents occurred in the vicinity where Parleigh was walking.

Once his man warned him away from the entrance of one of San Francisco's many underpasses. Parleigh stopped walking and turned away. Within seconds, he looked back in time to see two men fighting with knives moving toward the entrance.

Another time Parleigh fell from a pier during a vacation. He did not then know how to swim, but his man appeared and literally gave him instructions on how to keep afloat until he was saved by passersby.

While living in Los Angeles, Parleigh befriended a couple. His man did not approve of this friendship and let him know it in no uncertain terms. This time, however, Parleigh went against his man and maintained the relationship. His man took matters into his own hands, creating havoc whenever Parleigh was with them. The environment behaved as if poltergeists had invaded it. Windows would fly open or suddenly close. Objects fell from their places without being touched. Eerie sounds echoed through the house whenever Parleigh was there. The couple decided not to see Parleigh again. A short time later, he learned of their arrest. They had been convicted of dealing in drugs, an activity Parleigh had known nothing about.

"Parleigh," I asked him once, "in what other ways, besides protecting you, has your man been good to you?"

"Well," Parleigh answered with a smile, "in many ways. He has told me where to send manuscripts, who would accept my work. He's given me ideas and themes for many of my published stories. Before I was successful, I was always aware of him guiding me. Since I have become more successful, my man has not appeared as much. I suspect that he was mainly here to protect me and to guide me in a writing career."

I asked him if his man had ever shown himself to anyone else.

"Yes, to my sister. In fact, for some reason I did not see my man for a period of about eighteen months. During that time he visited my sister on various occasions. She thought she was going mad. Kept telling me about my man 'popping up all over the place,' as she put it. He did rap or knock, warning her that he was about to appear, which I think is good sport, don't you?" Parleigh's sense of humor is constant and crisp.

"One night I had a dream that my sister was in grave danger. My man was present during this dream. In it I saw someone grab my sister as she was walking. He seemed to be lurking behind some hedges as she came by. I didn't think much of it for my sister drives everywhere; I just couldn't imagine her walking. I didn't do anything about it. But several days later, I learned that my sister's car had broken down one day and that she had indeed had to walk to her destination. A man had leapt out of the bushes and grabbed her, but she had screamed until the neighbors came out and saved her. Had I been more in tune with my man, I could have warned her. I've always found that when I do not pay attention to my man, I get into trouble."

Parleigh related other incidents involving his man and other people. "On one particular afternoon, my man decided to show himself to a visitor I had at my apartment. We were having a midday cocktail when my man suddenly appeared. I wasn't sure that my friend could see him—that is, until he paled, got up from the chair, and actually hid behind it. I had to contain myself, it was really quite a funny sight. A grown man behind a chair. My man left and my guest came out, satisfied that the thing he saw was gone. When asked to describe the spirit, my friend did so, in perfect detail."

There was a similar occurrence when Parleigh was a guest in the home of a friend, a painter. Again, without warning, the spirit showed himself to the startled friend. Parleigh, curious to see if his friend saw his man in the same way he had, asked him what the entity looked like and what garments he was wearing. The painter did better than that. He went to his easel, took a fresh canvas, and began a quick painting of the ghostly visitor.

As the sketch neared completion, Parleigh saw that it was indeed his man. Just before the artist completed the last strokes, his hand was thrust up and down over the canvas. The brush he was holding ruined the likeness.

Parleigh heard his man's voice saying, "I don't wish to be painted!"

"I didn't do that," the artist exclaimed. "Something, or someone, pushed my hand across the painting!"

From his childhood Parleigh did not get along with his father. After he had grown up, during a reading by a clairvoyant, Parleigh was told that his father would become "one of the living dead." He thought it a most unusual expression to use.

Months later, Parleigh's father was involved in a horrible accident, and in the following two years, he did indeed live a deathly life. During this time Parleigh decided to get to know and better understand his father. "My karmic debt to my father was paid back during those months."

His man visited Parleigh one day and told him that his father would die later that day. Parleigh's father did die that afternoon.

The circumstances under which Parleigh's man has appeared to him are numberless. Parleigh was having a violent argument with another man once. His adversary began choking him. Parleigh's man showed himself at that moment, and the fight ended abruptly.

Parleigh accepts this entity completely, as if he were an actual, living person. The force has proven itself to be a good one. Parleigh has been protected, guided, and enlightened by him. Of all the experiences I have either witnessed or investigated, this is the most extensive case of what would commonly be referred to as a ghost story.

And now I can say that finally I have seen Parleigh's man with my own eyes. One day Parleigh and I were talking quietly at my home. Suddenly the temperature in the room dropped considerably. I sensed that something other than the two of us was here. Then I caught a quick glimpse of his man. I was neither startled nor frightened. In fact, an air of peace and quiet accompanied the being from another level.

I do not think that Parleigh J. Cooper's experiences with his man are unique. Almost anyone can conjure up a spriit—once one gains the proper instruction—if one decides to set himself to the task. As in Parleigh's case, there are spirits, or ghosts, who will attach themselves to persons without having been invited. Usually, the people are so frightened that the entity will cease trying to communicate after a period of time.

In my own life, I have been confronted by ghosts on three separate occasions. These three entities came to me in the same form in which they had lived on earth. I did not conjure them up; they sought me out and afforded me guidance or protection without my asking for their assistance.

The first experience was astonishing, to say the least. I was living in a trailer home in New Jersey. It was the middle of winter. On retiring, I had placed my silk Japanese robe at the foot of my bed. Sometime during the evening, I was awakened by the sound of movement in the trailer.

Startled—I was alone at the time—I sat up in bed. Across the room, in a corner, stood a man. He was dressed in flowing garments and wore a kind of turban on his head. The intruder spoke, addressing me in a clear, very human voice. I was instructed to place my right foot on the floor. Convinced that he was a dangerous robber, I immediately obeyed the command.

I slid my foot out from beneath the covers and onto the floor, where it came to rest upon my robe. The robe had slipped off the bed while I was asleep and had landed on the floor on one of the heating vents of the trailer. The heat pouring up from the vent was blocked by the robe, and had almost caused the garment to burst into flames. I kicked it across the floor.

When I looked up, the stranger was gone. Whoever he was, he had come to warn me of the fire that most assuredly would have taken place had I not noticed the robe at the exact moment that I did.

The second time that I was saved by a supernatural force was when I was traveling by car and trailer throughout the South. On this occasion, I had two traveling companions. It was late at night and the roads were curving and uninviting. I was in the back seat of the car. Suddenly, I felt the presence of someone other than the three of us. I turned and saw the same being that had visited me before. This time he said, "Put your seat belts on." He repeated this statement twice.

Forewarned, I told my friends of the visitor and his command. Understanding my psychic ability, they fastened their belts. Before an hour had passed, our driver swerved to avoid a dog that had sprung out onto the highway. The car turned over three times, landing in a swamp. We were hurt, but none of us was killed, a fact which amazed the local police. The damage to the car was so extensive that it seemed a miracle not one of us was dead.

"Those seat belts saved your lives," the sheriff was to tell us. "No doubt about it, you sure were lucky to have them fastened!"

The interesting thing to note here is that before the spirit addressed me, I had never worn seat belts.

The force had saved our lives. Later it became clear to me that this entity was one of my spiritual guides, a soul from beyond who is meant to instruct, protect and guide those of us on earth who would accept him as a reality. I think that everyone has such guides from the other stide, but that most people choose not to accept them as real. If they do happen ever to chance upon a spirit, most become so frightened that they make further confrontations impossible—if it's a force from beyond, then the thing must be evil. I am continually asked how to differentiate between an evil spirit and a good one. The answer, naturally, is that if the entity does good, then it is good force; and if it does bad, it is bad. By their fruits ye shall know them.

Sometimes supernatural visitors merely want to be recognized as such, and in fact can be quite playful. When I purchased my house in the country, I discovered that it was what some might call haunted. In redecorating the place I began to lose screwdrivers. For weeks, one screwdriver after another would disappear. At first, I thought it to be a case of absentmindedness. However, after the loss of the eighth screwdriver, I decided that someone was playing a trick on me. But the persons helping me were not responsible. It became a joke with the salesman in my local hardware store. I bought and lost twelve screwdrivers, all told. It was quite disconcerting.

The downstairs of the house had one bedroom which I converted into a study. But try as I might, I could not write in this room. Although its decor was bright and cheery, I felt depressed and rather cold whenever I entered it. The vibrations were strange.

After a time, the missing screwdrivers began to reappear, and in the most obvious places. I'd open the door to let the dog out and there on the doorstep would be a screwdriver. If they had been only misplaced, I certainly would have come across them before this. About ten screwdrivers turned up in a month's time.

Because of the case of the missing screwdrivers and the strange vibrations of the study, I knew that an entity was loose in the house. On several other occasions, I caught glimpses of something that would dart quickly out of my field of vision.

I meditated on the matter and decided to address the

unearthly being. I told it that I understood it wanted to be identified, and if it were earthbound, it should seek its true existence on a higher level—my moderate attempt at exorcism. I never was frightened by this entity; it was benign, albeit annoying. It did not show itself again after I spoke to it.

Almost a year passed before I found out that the father of the previous owner of the house had lived with the family. He had used the downstairs bedroom, now the study, and he liked to putter around the house, being mechanically inclined. There was no doubt in my mind that this man was the being who had visited me when I took over the house. I now feel that he has been released. I am no longer troubled by the entity and am quite able to work in the study. In fact, I sometimes feel a presence whenever I have to do some task that requires mechanical or physical dexterity, which I do not have naturally.

Since the writing of the above paragraphs, however, several of my house guests have been bothered by this "ghost." My mother, the last person I would imagine believing in such things as spirits or ghosts, was sleeping in one of the upstairs bedrooms on a recent evening. She was suddenly awakened by a sound at her door, which flew open as she began to rise up in bed. She said that something flying very fast zoomed over the right side of her head and touched her face before it left via the closed window! My mother now sleeps with the light on when she visits my home.

One evening, Eileen Dent and her daughter Roxanne, who were my house guests at the time, had gone to sleep in this same bedroom. Roxanne woke up as she felt something sit on the edge of her bed. Thinking it my dog, Bambi, she didn't pay much attention to it, until she heard Bambi on the other bed. Roxanne called out to her mother, "Mom, do you have Bambi in bed with you?"

"Yes," Eileen answered. "Why?"

"Because there's something sitting on my bed." Roxanne was now frightened.

Eileen switched the lamp on. There was nothing in the room. However, there was an indentation left on the bedspread where Roxanne had felt something. Both women stayed up the rest of the night. At one point, they heard someone or something outside the window rapping and knocking. The bedroom they were in is two stories off the ground.

On yet another occasion, some other guests heard a commotion in the hallway outside this very bedroom, which is down the hallway from my own. They said that they heard someone walk out of my room, close the door, and walk into the bathroom. For some reason they got up, went to the door, and called out to me in the bathroom, "Daniel, are you all right?"

Needless to say, they were shocked beyond belief when I answered from my own room, behind a closed door. When I got up and went to the bathroom, my guests pleaded with me not to open the bathroom door, as they were convinced that someone had gone in there. I opened it and, of course, there was no physical being in the room.

The only thing I can figure out is that this entity still remains in the house and for some reason is attacking those who are my guests rather than me directly. I now ask my guests to say a prayer of protection before they stay over.

My own experiences, with beings from another plane of existence, prove to me that not only do such entities exist, but that they also can return to the earth to do good. Spirits or ghosts have too often been ascribed evil motives—but they can prove to be positive forces as well.

CHAPTER 8

WHEN ORAL ROBERTS EXHORTS, COAXES, AND INSPIRES TO health people in his audience, when they stand up healed of minor and major afflictions, what really happens? Roberts and many others, famous and obscure, are utilizing a psychic force to heal those in need. It is an energy not of this world. The faith healers have grown in number. The work of Jesus in healing through faith is being increasingly remembered by contemporary Christian churches, who are tuning in to healing power as an answer to the countless illnesses of mind, body, and spirit which plague mankind now more than ever before.

There are numerous, well-publicized cases of fraud, but that should not obscure the fact that psychic healing *can* really work. The copious evidence since primitive times of the power of faith in healing includes the temples of Aesculapius in Greece, and, of course, both Old and New Testament stories of "miracle cures."

Healing is a form of white magic. It is the reverse side of the black-magic curse and practices such as voodoo. It comes about when the healer submits himself to the forces of good in the universe, which in turn work through him to create harmonious conditions, either physical or mental.

My first encounter with the phenomenon of spiritual healing occurred at about the same time that I was introduced to the occult. I was living in Hartford, Connecticut, and had befriended a dear lady there named Mae Aitken. It was because of her that I first began to investigate matters of psychic phenomena.

We used to spend hours discussing her religion, Spiritualism. The main aspects of this religion are communicating with those who have died and healing those who are in need on the earth plane.

"I've got healing power," Mrs. Aitken told me. "I've known it for a long time, and I use it quite often."

"What's healing power?" I asked.

"Using the power of God to make those who are sick well," she replied simply. "Everyone has a spiritual gift. You've been blessed with a very pronounced psychic ability. My gift is healing."

We talked about her ability for some time, and although she tried to explain to me what she was able to do, I wasn't convinced or satisfied that she could bring about well-being in those who were ill.

But she had a chance to prove herself to me when one morning I awakened to discover that I could hardly walk. I had been teaching dancing at the time and remembered vaguely that I had been kicked by another dancer. My right ankle was inflamed and I experienced excruciating pain. The vein just above my ankle was swollen and throbbing.

As the days passed, the condition became worse. The

pain was unbearable. My ankle was swollen to almost twice its normal size. I went to the doctor, who, to my dismay, gave me something more to worry about—it seemed that my vein had been damaged. He suggested an operation.

I told Mrs. Aitken about my condition, and she said, "You don't need an operation, Daniel. I'll take care of it."

"But," I protested, "the doctor says that it is important I have an operation or else I might not walk, or I might have a limp the rest of my life."

Mrs. Aitken smiled and said, "Please, give me a chance before you do anything."

I truly did not believe that she or anyone else could bring about healing. "Isn't it important that the one being healed believes that he can be healed, that he has faith in the healer?" I asked, betraying my limited background in metaphysics.

"Just let me try. You don't have to do anything, except to stop being so negative." Mrs. Aitken's staunch New England upbringing wasn't going to allow her to take no for an answer.

"O.K." I gave in. "But if there isn't any improvement, I'm going back to the doctor."

Although my psychic ability has been pronounced since childhood, so has a terrifying fear of pain, be it mental or physical. I have purposefully avoided pain of all kinds in my life, even at the occasional expense of spiritual progress. During the few years that I was a Christian Scientist, I found it impossible to do away with my dread of physical pain. "If there is indeed no such thing as pain," I remember asking the Christian Science practitioner whom I had sought out for advice, "then why does the Christian Science religion spend most of its time denying its existence? If, in truth, pain and sickness do not exist, they would not have to be refuted. Why attack something which doesn't exist in the first place?" The questions, I felt, were never answered properly.

I was therefore quite dubious about Mae Aitken's healing ability, but I nevertheless permitted her to try. Like most people in need, at this point I would have turned to anything.

Mrs. Aitken initiated a procedure at our first healing session that was repeated on many succeeding visits. She welcomed me into her living room, made tea, and had me relax. I sat on the sofa as Mrs. Aitken made herself comfortable in a chair opposite me. Shoe and sock removed, my foot rested across her lap. She removed all her jewelry and placed her right hand directly over the swollen ankle. Several prayers were said, and then Mrs. Aitken asked me to sing a hymn with her.

"I don't know any hymns," I said. "We don't sing hymns in the Catholic religion I was raised in."

Mrs. Aitken explained that a hymn was important because it brought up the vibrations, lifting the energy of the healer and the one being healed. She taught me several hymns. I acceded to her wish, although the intellectual part of my mind kept repeating that what was happening was hogwash.

After a few inharmonious hymns, Mrs. Aitken placed her right hand on the ankle. She passed her hand over the afflicted area, back and forth, ever so lightly. I immediately sensed heat emanating from her hand. On every succeeding healing session, I would sense this instant heat which her hand generated. It wasn't just body heat, or heat caused by the friction of rubbing. At times, it became almost as hot as a heating pad, and I would have to ask Mrs. Aitken to remove her hand for a few moments.

During the session Mrs. Aitken went deeper and deeper into what seemed a self-induced semitrancelike state. Her head bobbed up and down; and at times, when I spoke to her, there would be no forthcoming answer. If it were not for the constant hand motion, I would have surely thought her to be asleep.

The pain I experienced after our initial healing session was even more pronounced than it was before Mrs. Aitken laid hands on me. I brought this to her attention. "That's because the energies working on the condition through my hands are most powerful. It's almost like performing an operation, and that would be painful afterward, wouldn't it?"

I had no answer to this seeming insanity. This woman is strange, I thought. My leg feels as if it may fall off, and she tells me that's because it's getting better. It's crazy.

After the third or fourth session, the swelling and pain began to abate. Midway through these meetings, I heard a loud rapping on a small, round oak table in one corner of the room. The knocking was loud and clear. After demonstrating to myself that there was no material explanation for the noises, I asked Mrs. Aitken about them.

"Those are my spirit guides, telling us that they are here. They rap anytime I am doing a healing, and often when I'm meditating or sending healing to my loved ones by prayers."

After the rapping, I sensed a change in temperature in the room. It came as waves of cold and then hot wafts of air. Having only recently been awakened to the mere idea of psychic phenomena, I was, to say the very least, quite frightened by the odd happenings in Mrs. Aitken's apartment.

But it was not long until my ankle began to improve. I felt better after each of our meetings. In a two-month period, Mrs. Aitken administered approximately ten healings. In the third month the ankle was completely healed, the pain and swelling never to return again. The vein of the damaged foot is still a bit larger than the corresponding one on the other foot; yet, though I have continued dancing since that time, not once has any discomfort returned.

Through the years I have seen Mae Aitken work on everything from headaches to tumors. More importantly, she has been most successful with those who have sought her power of healing. Now retired from healing activities, she remains a remarkable woman. And, like most persons with a pronounced spiritual gift, she has never been able completely to explain her ability.

"It's God's work," she'd say quite often. "I've nothing to do with it. The power I use is that of a good force, the utilization of an unseen energy which is good and is meant to bring about well-being. Maybe it's because I have complete faith in the healing power I have, but I know that it is not I who does it, rather the force of good, God."

I've since been acquainted with several others in my life who have healing ability. Eileen Dent has a very pronounced capacity to heal. She had not known of this ability before I met her. When I psychically perceived healing power in her, she was startled to learn of it. Against her own feelings on the subject of faith healing, Eileen has involved herself many times in letting this power be used to accomplish good. Eileen has healed me on several occasions, reducing severe stomach pains, soothing burns and making them heal more quickly, and more. I've been witness to other healings she has performed as well. In Rochester, New York, to lecture to the Spiritual Frontiers Society there, I was to be introduced to the audience by one of the members of the group. The man had been ill with a fever and a sore throat. When it came time to go out onto the stage, he could hardly speak.

"Eileen will heal you," I said.

As she usually does, Eileen drew back at first and said that she could not heal. But after some prodding, she conceded and laid hands on the man. In a way similar to Mrs. Aitken's, Eileen concentrated deeply on the area that needed healing. She said a prayer of sorts and, as she herself often puts it, she "let go and allowed the higher forces to enter into my body and do the work." Within several minutes the man was able to go out onto the stage and introduce me, his sore throat completely gone.

I am aware that, as in the cases of Mae Aitken and Eileen Dent, those who do have healing power generate a tremendous amount of heat in their hands. Both Mrs. Aitken and Eileen have explained to me that they can feel this heat throughout their bodies. Sometimes they begin to perspire while in the midst of healing.

Science has begun to investigate the healing energies of those who possess this ability. In Russia, for example, scientists have developed a supersensitive photographic method which can record the electrical field that surrounds all living things—humans, animals, and plants. To those involved in spiritual work, this electrical field is known as the aura.

Several interested American scientists have taken up this kind of picture taking, known as Kirlian photography. Thelma Moss, of the Neuropsychiatric Institute at the University of California at Los Angeles, has studied various cases of psychic healings with this new photographic process. In the course of her investigations she came upon a most interesting detail. Miss Moss discovered that immediately following a healing, the healer's aura, or electrical field, decreased noticeably. However, the aura of the person being healed was greatly intensified. It appears that the vibrations of the healer are somehow passed on to the person being healed. Miss Moss also discovered that the fingertips of healers produced less electrical radiation when they were not being used for healing than when they were.

Douglas Dean of the Newark College of Engineering has also done extensive study in this area and has many Kirlian photographs to support the theory that electrical magnetic fields are passed from one person to another during healings.

The most extensive investigation of a specific psychic healer concerns a Brazilian peasant named Arigo. Dr. Henry Puharich of the New York University Medical Center and his research team examined many instances of healing administered by this uneducated man, who in 1971 was killed, at the age of forty-nine, in an automobile crash.

Arigo's healings were internationally known, and he had become a legend before his death. He said that the voice of a long-deceased physician guided him in the unorthodox methods of healing which he utilized. Arigo treated two hundred to three hundred patients a day. He performed minor surgery with a simple, unsterilized pocketknife. He recommended drugs for other persons, writing out prescriptions for unusual pharmacological combinations that were somehow effective.

There wasn't a known ailment on which Arigo did not work, and the majority of his patients survived, either recovering completely or at least showing marked improvement after the healings were administered.

Dr. Puharich studied firsthand more than one thousand of Arigo's cases. He was not able to discover any scientific explanation for the way in which Arigo made his diagnoses or, more importantly, how his healings were effective. The advanced scientific tools that Dr. Puharich used for his investigation proved beyond a reasonable doubt that actual healing had taken place under the most unbelievable circumstances. Dr. Puharich is now devoting much time to further research of psychic healing.

The most noted of psychic healers was the renowned,

late Edgar Cayce, but his work was more in the nature of diagnosing conditions and prescribing natural, herbal cures, rather than the one-to-one physical contact between healer and subject.

Captain Edgar D. Mitchell, who has been described as the "most intellectual of all the astronauts" by the majority of NASA observers, has done a great deal to further interest in psychic healing in America. His recent lecturing in healing is proving to be more of a boon to the world of psychic phenomena that even the highly publicized telepathy tests which he ran during the Apollo 14 flight.

"Psychic healing is an observable fact, and I have documented a number of cases clinically before and after treatment," Captain Mitchell told a number of interviewers before he acted as moderator at a conference held in Lincoln Center in the spring of 1973, entitled "Psychic Healing: Myth into Science."

Mitchell doesn't know where this healing energy, that so many people seem to have, comes from, but he is convinced that it is probably some kind of energy (consciousness energy) with a universal nature. From his own observations, Mitchell claims that this energy is as real as any of the other energies science has tried to understand.

"I suspect that in pre-scientific times gravitational, magnetic, and later electromagnetic energy must have seemed just as etheric," Captain Mitchell was quoted as telling the press.

At the same conference, Mitchell paid tribute to Dr. M. Justa Smith, a biochemist who has done extensive work and research in psychic healing. Dr. Smith successfully carried out experiments demonstrating that under a healer's hands the activity of human enzymes (important to body healing processes) in a vial is greatly increased.

"The healing energy might be channeled by the focusing of thought processes," Mitchell said. This was after he had done his own research on a young American who practices a most successful healing technique based on an ancient Tibetan meditative method. "The overriding concept is that all these events seem to be under the control of mind, and that by properly understanding mind, or consciousness, and its functions we'll come closer to understanding the nature of man."

Now that science is finally taking the idea of psychic healing more seriously, it is possible that psychic-healing centers may soon exist. The American Medical Association's recent downgrading of the ancient practice of acupuncture, however, indicates that most unorthodox methods of healing will take a long time to be accepted. In the past fifteen years, Dr. Jean Borsrello, a French air force physician, has developed a method of acupuncture with which he has treated more than four thousand patients with great success. He has stated that even though he cannot completely explain how acupuncture works, in physiological terms, this is no reason to prevent its use. The fact that acupuncture works is reason enough to use it in cases of illness. The same reasoning should apply to psychic healing. We shall see.

CHAPTER 9

THE THEATER DARKENS. LIGHTS OF SPELLBINDING EFFECT and music louder than the human ear can endure heighten the sense of frenzied anticipation which has come over the twenty thousand or more members of this audience. The majority of the crowd are teen-agers, some much younger.

Drugs are being openly sold and taken. Not only marijuana, but every conceivable kind of drug—pills, opium, hash, even the lethal heroin. One can see from a cursory glance about the mobbed auditorium that a large portion of these children are stoned out of their minds. They sit, heads bobbing up and down, trying to keep alert and "with it," at least until their idol goes into his first number. With a deafening crescendo, Alice Cooper arrives onstage. The crowd freaks out en masse; they become almost as wild and frightening as the performer they have shelled out huge sums of money to see. The tickets incidentally were sold out within hours of the mere announcement that Alice Cooper's rock group was coming to town.

This isn't New York, Chicago, or Los Angeles, but rather a small city in New Jersey. No matter where he goes—the Midwest, the South, either coast—Alice Cooper draws them by the tens of thousands.

His costume is many-faceted, consisting of a sequined, sleeveless T-shirt, a one-legged pair of the tightest pants, a fur piece around his neck, red boots, and a silver American Indian belt.

In repose, offstage, Alice Cooper's face would be almost handsome if it didn't have a drawn, debauched look and an aura that suggests melancholy, sadness, death. Death is one of the important aspects of Alice Cooper's performance.

Onstage, Alice Cooper could pass for the character Death as portrayed on the appropriate Tarot card. His eyes are outlined by heavy black makeup, which covers the entire upper lids and part of the cheeks. Black, clown-like tears fall beneath the eyes. The lines at the corner of the mouth are also outlined in black. Someone in the mob yells, "Wow! He looks like the Devil!" It's an apt description.

The music played by Alice Cooper's group is discordant, loud, frantic, and difficult, even to those who enjoy rock. It is acid rock at its most illustrative. The lyrics (if one has the chance to see them in print, for they cannot ever be understood in performance) create the worst possible images. They conjure up thoughts that are not only ugly but obscene.

Let me put something straight here. I love rock music—from the Beatles, to Paul Simon, to the Moody Blues. I find that we do not have poets today, we have rock-lyric writers in their place. The words of most rock writers are inspiring, filled with compassion for the human soul, and genuinely uplifting. They will endure as long as language. This, therefore, is no criticism of rock music or of the performing arts. It is, however, a criticism and a direct condemnation of the horror now being perpetrated on large masses of children in the guise of music and entertainment.

The nineteen-seventies ushered in the extreme forms of avid rock and with them all the inhuman, degrading, self-destructive elements that characterize the kids who use hard drugs. Alice Cooper's performance exemplifies these elements. It reeks of hate, violence, and human despair. A sadomasochistic relationship exists between Alice and his audiences. What he does onstage is designed to evoke evil, and it is successful.

When his group performs its hit "Dead Babies," Alice actually chops up the lifelike mannequin of a child and throws the dismembered pieces to the audience. They scream for more.

Alice comes down into his audience and grabs the hair of several kids. This he does not do gently. When pain is expressed by those whose hair is being pulled, Alice lets go. The kids fight one another to have Alice Cooper inflict physical pain on them.

Alice either fakes or in actuality kills live chickens onstage. He bites off their heads and drinks their blood, or seems to.

One of his props is a live boa constrictor which Alice uses in vile ways. In England, the Alice Cooper group appeared on that nation's most popular television musical/variety show, 'Tops For Pops." The boa constrictor crawled all over Alice's body, finally discovering and entering a strategically ripped hole in his costume, near the crotch. Alice mimed sexual release as the snake became entwined in and around his genitals. The secretary of the National Viewers and Listeners Association of Great Britain issued statements condemning this performance. "This man is both violent and anarchic," she said.

In interview after interview, Alice Cooper is referred to offstage as a gentle, peaceful, kindly person, completely unlike the sadistic monster which takes over the stage at performance time and hypnotizes masses of children into senseless, hopeless, and defiled states. Possibly he *is* really a "nice guy." Possibly he is merely the creation of managers and/or agents who know the pulse of the times and will offer any form of debauched insanity to make money off the kids. What with best-selling records, sold-out concerts, and TV appearances, it is estimated that Alice Cooper's group now takes in millions of dollars annually.

Alice torments his audience. He showers them with disdain, even hatred. His sexuality is ambiguous. Half the time he appears to be completely effeminate, the other half he is very masculine, albeit sadistically so. He projects sex in the most flagrant manner, extolling complete promiscuity and perversity.

At the end of each performance, Alice Cooper is "killed." His feigned death often comes as he is "hanged" onstage. This is the most important aspect of his performance. The audience is beside itself with joy as his eyes roll, his tongue hangs out, and he kicks the air like a person dying of strangulation. Whether it is the killing of chickens or his own faked demise, violence and death seem to be what Alice Cooper is all about.

"This whole generation is bent on self-destruction," Alice Cooper told an interviewer from *After Dark* magazine. "Self-destruction is great! It's fun! I don't plan to be thirty. I just say to have fun, every day. If you have to answer to anyone for what you do, then you're really killing yourself."

Alice and his managers have compared his performance to an airplane crash. "People would come for miles to see dismembered parts of bodies. They'd even pay to see it." Alice feels he's giving his audiences what they want—simulated horror, self-destruction, death. Maybe he is. Many of his performances have ended in near-riots, and although a lot of kids get hurt, they don't seem to mind. They dig it. They seem to groove on this ugliness, pain, and death.

Are the devil-like image and the evil onstage goings-on of Alice Cooper an accident, a sick joke? Or can it be that an evil force is utilizing him, a truly demonic force, that means to ensnare children into becoming its sadistic, drug-laden victims—those kids who are unable to care or feel except when mental or physical pain is inflicted on them?

I am completely convinced that there are many persons involved in the arts today who have become—some knowingly, others unwittingly—emissaries of the evil force that is out to grab as many of us as it can, in any way it can. It is said that the arts reflect the times and presage the future. If that is so, then we are all in for a lot of trouble.

I went to a well-touted evening of occultism and magic at Madison Square Garden in New York City. The prepared acts were quite interesting, though mostly of the sensational, show-biz type.

One of the main events of this particular evening was a centuries-old magic trick—the sawing in half of a woman. As the magician began to saw his victim in two, she suddenly let out a bloodcurdling scream. The audience froze and instantly went silent. The electric saw continued as the magician frantically tried to stop it. Too late. Blood issued from the box in which the woman had been placed. In a second's time the box was cut in two, the top half of the woman in one section, her legs in the other. The audience thought it had witnessed a horrible accident.

After a few moments the magician turned to the crowd

and announced that it had been a fake, a trick. The lady wasn't dead, she hadn't been cut in two. He asked members of the audience to come forward. Many did. As they realized that they had been taken in by a trick, many began to shout words of dismay at the magician. A number of people were upset because the lady had not been actually murdered in front of their eyes!

"God! I thought we had seen something really exciting."

"What a cheat, make-believe blood and guts. He really had me going for a minute. I should have known better."

"Fake! Rip-off! Bum!"

It is in the late nineteen-sixties. I have gone to the theater, an Off Broadway play. It is a new piece by a woman writer who has come to the fore with a very successful first play. Tonight is Thursday, usually a quiet day for Off Broadway. However, in this theater almost every seat is taken. Several newspapers have given the play excellent reviews.

The setting is a jungle which extends out into the audience. Vines, flowers, and trees wind up posts and across the ceiling. The play begins. Nude men walk around to the beat of drums. The plot concerns, I think—as it is difficult to discern the action—a white woman who somehow manages to become a goddess figure to a group of natives in Africa. Another character is a ghoulish-looking man who, I believe, represents Christ. He dies by strangling himself onstage, naked, with all the physical ugliness and torment a real death would have. It takes about ten minutes for him to die—his eyes roll, his mouth spews foaming saliva, and his face undergoes a series of mortal grimaces that deserve prizes for disgusting horror. During his dying scene, the man manages an erection, something he has been incapable of earlier in the play!

So far the evening has been filled with the most contemptuous and odoriferous writing, directing, and acting. Patiently, I wait for the end, which is not in sight. I don't want to offend the five people who have accompanied me to the theater tonight.

Now a ritual scene. A live goat is brought onstage, and members of the cast dance to the sacrificial music. A razor-sharp knife is held high above the goat as it is placed on a wooden block. The music begins a crescendo. Suddenly the onstage lights go black for several seconds. In the darkness the live goat is quickly replaced by a stuffed one. It happens so neatly that most of the audience are unaware of the substitution.

Just as the lights come up full onstage, the poised knife sweeps down and rips open the stomach of the goat. Innards (probably purchased at the nearest chicken market) burst forth from the gaping belly. The white goddess then picks up the innards and begins to rub them on her body, and then to chew on them!

I can stand no more. Jumping to my feet, I yell at the actors on the stage, telling them that they should be ashamed of themselves for demeaning not only their acting abilities and the theater but themselves as well. I race up the aisle to the nearest exit. The audience gives me a burst of applause. I stand in the lobby waiting for my friends, who must be embarrassed beyond belief.

I don't know that the playwright is in the audience this night. As I stand in the lobby she walks past me, apparently aware that I am the person who has disrupted her play.

"It's too bad you don't understand or appreciate art, young man," she says.

"That may be true. However, I do understand what *you* are doing, only too well," I reply. "And I think you should seek professional help immediately."

Later, I ask my friends if I have been too harsh or overdramatic in my severe reaction to the play. But none of them has been able to make any sense out of the evening, other than that it has afforded the playwright an opportunity to create onstage a part of her mind that is spiritually and emotionally bleak, half-crazed, and quite dead.

In 1966 I was one of a vast crowd that attended the lecture/performance (or theatrical happening, as it was billed) of Timothy Leary at the Santa Monica Civic Auditorium in California. This massive place (where Academy Award ceremonies have been held) was sold to capacity for the five scheduled Leary appearances.

There was rock music, a light show, ritual dancing, and chanting. A contingent of Leary's followers were onstage with him during the performance, all of whom seemed to be stoned out of their minds.

Leary seemed, to me at least, a sorry example of a hippie gone over the hill. His talk was so naïve and blunt that I don't know whether it was what he said or how he said it that angered me more.

Leary openly advocated the taking of drugs—all kinds of drugs. He equated drug taking with the highest form of spiritual enlightenment that one can have. He said that drugs should be used as a blessed sacrament and that LSD was "the Christ of the twentieth century," meant to offer enlightenment and freedom just as Jesus had done almost two thousand years ago. Leary spoke of revolution, through violent methods. He told the kids never to listen to their parents, or to anyone else who might be in a position to have any power over them (he excluded himself from this latter group, however).

The audience vibrations were palpable. It was an atmosphere of reverence. The kids hung onto every word their guru said, as though they were hearing the divine Buddha.

As the audience filed out of the auditorium, I overheard several conversations.

"He really knows where it's at."

"That man is God-sent. I would follow him to the moon."

"Leary's right, you know, the establishment has got to be destroyed before we can build it into the heaven he knows it can be."

"If drugs have made him so open, so spiritual, so much a master, then he's for me! I just hope that I can reach the heights that he has."

It was an evening that left me frightened and very angry. I had the strong feeling that Leary had opened himself to lower entities through the use of drugs, and that Darker power was moving him to become the pied piper of LSD. It was the first time in my life that I had ever felt that someone should be physically stopped before he could destroy the thousands that perceived him as their master. Those performances encouraged the spread of the drug culture across the nation. And we know what has become of most of those kids who dropped out, took acid, and followed their hero—they are either leading destroyed lives, or are in institutions, or they are dead.

The theater is not the only branch of the arts in which the energies of evil choose to utilize their forces in reaching souls and deterring them from spiritual progress. All forms of art are being used by evil.

Vito Acconci is an artist. He is very successful, has received grants, and "has shown" in various well-known art galleries. He is involved in a new form of art called body art. This new approach to artistic endeavor might be thought ludicrous if it were not taken seriously by art critics and the public. Every major art magazine has carried articles about Acconci and his work, and he has been acclaimed for several years now.

His work resembles what the 'sixties called "happenings"—the artist uses his own body to "create." In 1970, for example, an Acconci exhibit consisted of art patrons watching him climb up and down an eighteen-inch-high stool until he was exhausted.

That was it!

Another Acconci work was displayed at a small theater he had rented. Seated onstage, alone, Acconci stared at each member of the audience for a period of fifteen seconds apiece.

Finis!

Videotapes play important roles in his work. On videotape he has done "sex-change exercises." In these he hides his penis between his legs and then, as he puts it, "I try to learn how to move as a female would."

Acconci is not alone in this madness called body art. Bruce Nauman has also shared acclaim in the use of videotapes of himself. One of his works, highly praised, is a tape of himself in his studio as he spreads his lips apart with his fingers. Another is of Nauman throwing himself against a wall and bouncing off it.

Terry Fox, another body artist, achieved his major work when he drew a circle with his own blood on a floor that had been covered with dirt. He then lay on his back in the center of the blood circle, clutching various tubes filled with blood, urine, milk, and water. He remained there for more than six hours, trying to levitate himself.

Other artists have been known to invite people to exhibitions of their work and then to perpetrate some form of horror on them. One stood in the middle of an empty gallery in a raincoat. As the guests came in and asked where the exhibition was, he would open his coat to reveal his nude body, penis erect. Another artist had his "work" inside a huge box in the center of the floor. As his well-heeled guests, some in evening dress, gathered around the roped-off box, the artist suddenly threw open the lid, grabbed plastic bags that had been filled with ox blood and chicken guts, and proceeded to throw them at the horrified spectators. The bags burst and in a few moments the entire crowd was covered with gore. "I want to make people feel," he said.

In an article about Acconci that appeared in *Saturday Review*, David Bourdon, a contributing editor, describes a particular work as "brilliant." The piece, entitled "Seedbed," was exhibited at the Sonnabend Gallery in 1972. In an empty room of the gallery there was a wooden ramp, under which Acconci had sealed himself. The art lovers entered the room and walked over the ramp. As they did so, Acconci moved from one part of the confined space to another, all the while indulging in private sexual activity, and, as he said, "scattering my seed throughout the underground area. In my seclusion I can have private images of the people walking over me, talk to myself about them, my fantasies about them can excite me, enthuse me to sustain or to resume my private sexual activity. The seed planted on the floor, then, is a joint result of my performance and theirs." Acconci carried a microphone with him, and what he said was broadcast over a speaker system as the exhibition was in progress. His words were obscene, and directly related to the reactions of those who were walking over him. Some persons became angry and stomped across the ramp, at which Acconci would cry out, in sexual ecstasy, "Oh, God, step on me. Step on me harder. You can do it, come on, baby!"

Literature has also been invaded by the forces that seek to demean and debase the positive aspects of human life. I don't think it is a coincidence that best-selling novels of the recent past have been such books as *Rosemary's Baby, The Other,* and *The Exorcist.* Each in its way deals with the Darker, more evil elements of the occult. Each of them is beautifully written. But, unfortunately, I have personally known many people who read these books and were turned onto some form of Satanism, witchcraft, or other forms of evil worship, some on merely a mental level, others involving themselves deeply in something they had little understanding of.

Children's books offer the best example of infiltration of literature by the lower forces. Editors and publishers, cognizant of what sells on the market, are as guilty as authors of spreading the evil present today.

Some of the current best-selling children's books deal with suicide, premarital sex, abortion, and drugs. If these books were positive in their approach, if they offered children insight into sociological problems they will undoubtedly have to face long before adulthood, then there would be honest justification for their existence. However, in most cases, these books either offer no enlightenment, other than fear, or else they are so farfetched, so extreme despite their realistic approach, that I feel they are providing the atmosphere for our very young that next leads them to the likes of Alice Cooper.

Jean Renvoize's *A Wild Thing* is an example of a successful children's book of this kind. Its plot concerns a young orphan girl named Morag. She has lived in foster homes most of her young life, but she runs away to the mountains. Morag makes a home for herself in a cave, having befriended a mountain goat and its kid. She eats by stealing from nearby farms and by killing game. One day she discovers the skeleton of a human near her cave. She decorates it with flowers and then commences to worship it.

Morag later comes to the scene of an accident. A man

has been killed in a fall, his skull split on a rock. Another man, his companion, lies dying. But Morag proceeds to nurse this man back to health. When he is well, he rapes her. After he has had his fill of her, he leaves her, returning to civilization by himself.

Morag is alone again on the mountain. Now she is pregnant. Winter is about to descend, and Morag knows that she doesn't have a chance of survival in the mountains. She seeks help and is attacked by the angry villagers, who realize that she is the one who has been robbing them. She is seriously wounded by them and barely makes her way to the seashore. Beside the ocean Morag has a miscarriage and then dies. She becomes a skeleton and her bones a part of the white sand. End of story.

Here is an excerpt from this children's story about Morag's hunting experience:

> *The rabbit was a perfect target. She swallowed, aimed and shot. . . .*
>
> *The rabbit screeched, jumped up into the air kicking wildly, somersaulted over backward, and fell down heavily to the ground. . . .*
>
> *It began to jerk wildly and scream out. Thrashing around in violent convulsions all the time it let out those piercing screams that filled the woods and sent the birds crashing through the young leaves in their alarm. . . .*
>
> *Finally pity gave her strength to summon herself, helped her to grab the frenzied thing, swing it up high and bring it down like a chopper onto the edge of the stump, so that its neck broke and at last it lay still, bloody and lifeless.*

Another popular contemporary children's book is *Wild in The World* by John Donovan. This book tells the story of the Gridley family, of which there are thirteen members, homesteaders in the hills of New Hampshire. The first pages of the book detail the deaths of many of the children in the family. These deaths are caused by fire, rattlesnake bites, suicide, scarlet fever, and other causes. On page 5 one son named Abraham has to rip a fish-hook from his hand. He contracts an infection and dies a few days later. On page 6 another son, Amos, is kicked in the groin by a cow and is dead soon afterward. Chapter One of *Wild in the World* closes with only John, another son, left alive. Later John makes friends with a wild animal, either a wolf or a dog that resembles a wolf. He teaches the animal tricks and then plans to join a circus. He truly loves the animal, which is bitten by a rattlesnake but survives after days of agony. John catches pneumonia, and the major part of this ninety-four-page book tells the reader of his slow, pitiful death.

Patrick Merla, in an article for *Saturday Review*, wrote: "Both *Wild in the World* and *A Wild Thing*, though excellently written, present an extreme realism in which although specific details are scrupulously, even meticulously, rendered, the situations are so extraordinary as to be out of the range of average experience." It may be that children's writers today steer purposely clear of fantasy in order not to mislead the young, but some critics obviously believe this "extreme realism" is perhaps more unhealthy for young readers.

Barbara Wersba's children's book entitled *Run Softly, Go Fast* illustrates how far we have come—and, I believe, in a negative way—from fairy tales and fables. Here is a short selection from this work:

> *"Marty was a dealer in dope and I was in the midst of Marty's entourage . . . Guys like Valiant who made cookies laced with pot and sold them in schoolyards. Girls like Happytime who balled anyone who would give her speed. Pale sick people who lived in communal pads and caught each other's lice and washed each other's backs in a dirty communal tub. Who got busted*

and went to jail for possession and got sprung and made the scene again. Who lived like paupers but had the best stereo systems in the world. Who lay around evenings on mattresses as the joint was passed from hand to hand, and the music blared, and the incense wafted from paisley wall to paisley wall. And whose parents were looking for them all over America . . . Clever Martin Brooks, playing father to little street junkies and fourteen year old derelicts because they put out for him, in more ways than one . . ."

In many of these children's books there isn't a glimpse of hope, there isn't a feeling of anything but hatred, violence, and death. When I was a child, I was frightened enough by the make-believe goblins and the adventures of those who lived in the stories I read—the Giant of "Jack in the Beanstalk" or the Wicked Witch of "Snow White and the Seven Dwarfs." Yet somehow I knew that they were just stories, and they did have positive attributes. I doubt that I could have contended with the brutal, ugly realism of modern children's literature. Either I would have become a recluse in the safety of my home, or I would begin to look into the things so ruthlessly, realistically portrayed, curious and vulnerable because of my inexperienced youth.

I have always loved motion pictures. They were my salvation when I was a child, escaping from a family and a life I didn't particularly enjoy. I believe that film is the most all-encompassing of art forms. Its recent moral degeneration reflects the decline of society, the same decline reflected in all the other art forms.

The biggest money-making film of all time is *The Godfather*. By the time you read this, it will have grossed more than a hundred million dollars at the box office. I found *The Godfather* to be the most demoralizing, violent, spiritually lacking, and destructive film ever produced. True, it is brilliantly written, directed, acted, and photographed; but its inherent evil overpowers everything else.

At the showing I witnessed, which was during the first week of its New York City premiere, the chic East Side theater was packed. The audience was caught up in this evil tale from the first frame and found itself siding with one Mafia "family" against another. The script is so brilliant that one doesn't immediately realize that every character in this film is a hate-filled, sadistic murderer. This is one of the films in which two or more sets of Bad Guys fight one another to the death. I felt they all would have been better off exterminated. I wasn't taken in for a moment; I couldn't help seeing evil in all the characters and didn't root for anyone. At the end, when Marlon Brando, who plays the Godfather, dies, I applauded. The audience turned and glared at me. He was the hero of the film and many people were openly sobbing at his demise. I couldn't believe it, for if one looks just a scratch beneath the surface of this story he quickly realizes that the character Brando portrays has reached the top not by being the quiet-spoken, soft-hearted, child-loving man that he plays at the end of the film. He had to be the biggest, strongest, and most violent of them all to reach that pinnacle.

A young black couple sat next to me during this screening of *The Godfather* and exemplified the reactions of most of the audience. They were titillated—they reacted to every shooting, every bit of violence, every hate-filled act as if they were watching a World Series ball game. That is, until the scene near the end when all the Mafia family heads come together and discuss whether they should become involved in the traffic of drugs or stay out of it. The leaders finally decide that it is the right thing to do, but only after promising one another that they will try to keep the sale of drugs in the ghettos of Harlem and such places, selling it to the "niggers," who "aren't human anyway," and making sure that their own children will not have immediate access to it.

The young black couple fell silent. I looked over at them and realized that the drug speech had truly hit home with them. It was as though friends they had come to understand and love and root for had betrayed them. It had touched their own lives and was no longer entertaining. They didn't stamp their feet and clap their hands when other members of the cast were knocked off, as they had been doing before all through the film. The stark, ugly, depraved reality of the piece was clear: they were all Bad Guys now. It was very interesting. I think that very few people had this reaction to the film.

Many of my friends who love and defend the film tell me that I should have viewed it as a truly epic motion picture, artistically one of the best ever made. "You should have gotten a lot of fun out of it, the excitement and all," one of my friends said to me. But I don't find *The Godfather* funny, exciting, or valuable, other than as a telling reflection of current attitudes about good and evil.

I had the same reaction to one of the most highly touted films of the nineteen-sixties, *Bonnie and Clyde,* which I found to be abhorrent in every conceivable way. How dare the film makers ask—demand—that the audience have compassion for these most horrible of murderers and their dastardly union?

And why should we have compassion for the unfeeling, degraded, self-destructive, and completely unhuman characters of *Last Tango in Paris*? Why should their ugliness be made mysteriously intriguing and even enticing to audiences who flee from it in real life? *Last Tango in Paris* is a lesson in physical, mental, and spiritual suicide, made to look in every technical way a work of art.

Deep Throat is a film about a lady who has a clitoris in

her esophagus. It was one of the most financially successful films of early 1973, before the Supreme Court finally ruled that it had no *raison d'être* either as a human study or an expression of art.

In looking over a recent edition of *The New York Times*, I found exactly twenty-two advertisements for films that were X-rated. Each of them is of the cheaply made, grossly violent, pornographic variety. I am not aesthetically opposed to such films, but you only have to read the ads to realize how the film medium is being used by the lower forces.

One ad states: "CARVED OUT OF TODAY'S HEADLINES! SEE THE SLASHING MASSACRE OF EIGHT (8) INNOCENT NURSES—SEE *SLAUGHTER HOTEL*, a place where nothing is forbidden." This despicable film, cashing in on the recent well-known murder case, was playing at two major motion-picture houses, not at an out-of-the-way porno house. In fact, a good portion of the twenty-two films advertised were being shown at major theaters.

Unlike many of my contemporaries in the occult professional world, I do not find sex to be evil. I believe that sex is a joyous expression of love and that there is no better means of communication between persons who do love one another. Therefore I am not condemning sex films per se. I do condemn films that debase women (or men, for that matter), placing them in roles that seek to degrade and make disgusting the art of love and/or sex. These films usually have a sadistic or masochistic bent. They are usually chauvinistic (like the aforementioned, supposedly artistic *Last Tango in Paris*, in which Maria Schneider is forced to submit to every kind of sexual congress with Marlon Brando, she completely nude while he remains dressed throughout).

Having seen several of these films myself, I must add

that I usually walk out—sex is one thing; depraved, violent filth is quite another.

The current popularity of super-macho black films is another reflection of widespread urges toward violence. Having a keen interest in the art of blacks, especially in the areas of drama and song, I went to several of these films. Every one of them had something in common—they all incited deep feelings of hatred and destruction toward whites, any whites, in their screenplays. I saw these films in New York City, among audiences who were, for the most part, black. Reactions by the blacks to these films, which openly condone and glorify the killings of whites (probably because the whites in the stories usually are guilty of tremendous wrongdoing), were the most overwhelmingly vicious I have ever witnessed. Fights, thrown objects, physical mayhem, and complete chaos usually ensued in the theaters which showed these films. I have often wondered if there was any connection between the rash of white-police or -civilian shootings and these films. If I were black and saw one of these films, I would, I think, seek some kind of revenge. The intent of these films is to rip off the black audience by showing Whitey getting his comeuppance, his due. Ironically, the producers of these films are never black.

We are fast becoming a society of people not unlike the unfeeling, negative, violent souls so brilliantly portrayed in Anthony Burgess's *A Clockwork Orange*. Instead of pointing the way toward a more positive, hopeful, and uplifting state of mind, all the art forms of today are utilizing the forces which tend to demoralize, weaken, and destroy. I believe that what we read, view, and otherwise take into our consciousness is what we eventually become. The human defilement which seems to be so much a part of the art world today is ammunition for the forces that seek to destroy us by leaving no avenue for spiritual rejuvenation. Enjoying this kind of art is one more way that we can lose control of our subconscious minds, affording those evil forces opportunities to take hold.

CHAPTER 10

A CASUAL SURVEY OF AMERICAN PERIODICALS IN THE LAST few years reveals an astonishing increase in numbers and kinds of articles about the occult. These stories describe what is happening, and they also reflect the seemingly insatiable public interest in the subject. The range of phenomena considered varies from the silly to the bone-chilling.

In the June 1, 1969, issue of the magazine section of *The New York Times* appeared one of the first articles to announce the widespread, epidemic proportions of college interest in matters related to the more ominous aspects of the occult. Both surprise and shock were expressed by the author, Dr. Andrew M. Greeley, about the extent and content of the occurrence he uncovered.

Greeley found that there was an organization on the campus of the University of Chicago operating under the name of WITCH. The letters stand for "Women's International Terrorist Corps from Hell." Members of this somber-sounding horde involve themselves in many areas of the occult; they have a sister organization on the West Coast which calls itself the California Druids. WITCH came to the attention of the public after staging numerous demonstrations on the college campus. It accused the social-science department of being backward in its approach to things that pertained to the supernatural and matters in general. Instead of circulating a petition or writing letters to the trustees, they registered their protest by casting a spell on the social-science department via a group hex.

Other items of interest that Greeley's article pointed out:

—A midwestern Catholic university discovered that an active coven of warlocks was present on campus. The dean of the school made the following statement to the press, "We've certainly come a long way. A couple of hundred years ago, we would have burned them at the stake. Twenty-five years ago I would have expelled them. Now, we attempt to reach them through psychiatry or other means which utilize the power of the mind."

—When they were asked to recommend subjects that they would like to be taught at their school, the majority of students at a renowned university in Canada suggested, in this order, astrology, Zen, sorcery, witchcraft, and other topics related directly or indirectly to the occult.

—The bookstore with largest volume of business in the Harvard area recently was one called the Sphinx Occult Bookstore.

—The *I Ching* method of supernatural divination (telling a fortune by throwing dice or coins and interpreting the particular sequence of resulting numbers) was a prime influence in the lives of hundreds of Catholic schoolgirls throughout the country.

Greeley also found that a vast number of dropouts from Berkeley in northern California had become members of "Six-Day School," an unorthodox establishment somewhere in the lush countryside of Sonoma. Its main teachings were political pacificism, astrology, mysticism, and magic. Students of the school had made field trips to Mt. Shasta in nearby Washington, long an American Indian sacred ground. At Mt. Shasta the Six-Day School pupils meditated, cast spells, and otherwise delved into the world of the supernatural.

Greeley's investigations demonstrated a number of harmless ways in which Americans had gone out to search for the thrills sometimes inherent in the occult. Time and again, however, research shows that many persons who do tread the paths of the unknown without protection experience horror or even death.

One such story, widely covered by the press, occurred in a small city called Vineland in New Jersey. Patrick Michael Newell was born and raised there. According to *Newsweek* magazine (July 19, 1971), Newell had a great interest in black magic and had made a collection of ancient occult rituals. He was known to have performed Satanic rites and had, furthermore, a documented death fixation, having once attempted suicide. His friends told reporters of his sadistic impulses. Newell would put a hamster in a wooden box into which sharp nails had been driven, then shake the box until the animal was pierced through many times. He spoke of these animal killings as ritual sacrifices.

Landis Park in Vineland was in recent years the site of devil-worship ceremonies performed by high-school students. The number of active devil worshipers was between eighty and ninety. A young housewife in Vineland, the mother of five children, admitted to meeting regularly every week with eight other middle-class Vinelanders. The group, she said, attempted witchcraft and performed rites of black magic. These practices came to light after the strange murder of Patrick Newell hit the headlines. Newell's body was found floating in a pool at the bottom of a sandpit, his arms and legs taped together.

Investigation led by the local police chief, Charles Pangburn, disclosed the fact that Vineland was not the peaceful town most of its residents thought it to be. The two murder suspects of Patrick Newell were arrested within a short time after the crime was uncovered. They had been friends of Newell, fellow students at Vineland High School. According to the suspects, Carl Sweikert and Richard Williams, Newell had asked to be killed. He had convinced them that he belonged to a sect of Satan worshipers and had to die violently before his soul could be put in charge of "forty leagues of demons."

At the time of his death, Newell was twenty years old, his murderers about the same age. He had asked them to kill him while attending a pregraduation party on June 13. His two accommodating friends taped his feet and hands together, carried out some form of ritual Newell had taught them, and then threw him into the pool where he drowned.

Williams and Sweikert were convinced that Newell would come back from the dead; and many Vinelanders were truly frightened, especially when the words "I'll be back" were found scrawled in his handwriting on a rustic lean-to he had built in the woods.

At the time of the Newell murder Judge George Shunk, of neighboring Franklyn Township, told investigators of the death that there had recently been a strange find in his area. A dozen or more dolls wrapped in black cloth and impaled, voodoo-style, by long sharp pins had been found tied to trees. The dolls had been imprinted with the names of various local women. The dolls were immediately destroyed.

A minister in Vineland, Reverend Snook, made this statement after the Newell murder was announced: "These kids are looking for something, they are so empty. Satan worship was just the next step beyond the drug fad, or, more correctly, something to go with drug taking."

Newsweek carried several follow-up articles about the rise of devil worship. In its August 16, 1971, issue the magazine estimated that "there are tens of thousands of Americans across the country, some of them middle class adults with advanced university degrees, who dabble in Satanism, witchcraft, voodoo and other forms of black or white magic."

In July, 1971, Kim Brown, a twenty-two-year-old avowed Satanist, rationalized her brutal murder of a sixty-two-year-old man by swearing that during a black-magic ceremony, the Devil had appeared and bidden her to commit the crime. After being convicted of murder and sentenced to a light term of seven years in prison, the young lady was quoted as saying, "I really enjoyed killing him. I had an orgasm while stabbing him."

A Los Angeles school teacher was murdered in 1970. The press reported later that her grave had been opened and the heart, lungs, and other parts of the body had been removed and used in a bloody ritualistic sacrifice to the Devil at the gravesite.

Newsweek recently quoted Father Richard Woods, a philosophy instructor at Chicago's Loyola University, as saying that there were over eighty thousand "white witches" in the United States. There were six thousand white witches in the Chicago area alone, Father Woods estimated.

One of the more bizarre news stories concerning the

occult appeared in the October 19, 1968, issue of *Illustrated Business Week.* Its topic was, not extraordinarily, Management versus Labor, but there was a new twist—witchcraft.

According to the article, the General Cigar Company was asking the National Labor Relations Board to void a collective-bargaining election that had been won by the National Association of Machinsts and Aerospace Workers, on the grounds that witchcraft had been used to influence the vote. The company said that countless union supporters at its plant in Puerto Rico had practiced witchcraft at the time of the election and had done so most successfully. Employees felt ill while voting, and many couldn't find the "no union" slot on the ballot. Many of the employees said that they could not remember how they had voted afterward, that they had been in a kind of daze.

The company went on to charge that a pro-union employee had purchased a bottle of something said to be a "magic potion" from a reputed sorceress, had induced fellow workers to smell the contents, and then had informed them that they could not vote against the union. Two persons who practiced witchcraft had been paid $150 each by union members to work for the company and induce fellow workers to join the union. The union won the election. The General Cigar Company asked the board to void the election on the grounds that the union had "exploited the workers' superstitions, thus preventing a free election."

The New York Times has seen fit to print many stories about strange happenings related to the occult. On January 6, 1969, *The Times* reported the story of Mrs. Francis Webb Smith, not only a teacher but the principal of the elementary school in Wetumpka, Alabama. Trustees of the Elmore County school had requested that Mrs. Smith submit her resignation after learning that she was teaching and practicing voodoo in the classroom. In all the schools in which she had previously taught, there had been similar complaints made against the sixty-two-year-old woman.

Back in 1966, *The Times* told of another voodoo incident, this one culminating in murder. Claude Morreiset, aged twenty-eight, and Mary Dutchaellier, fifty-five, who had known each other in Haiti since Morreiset was twelve, had become residents of New York City in the nineteen-sixties.

Mrs. Dutchaellier lived in an apartment building on West Ninety-sixth Street. One evening, the other tenants heard the sounds of arguing and fighting inside the Dutchaellier apartment.

"You have to cure me," a male voice shouted.

"I can't cure you," Mrs. Dutchaellier was heard responding.

"Then you are going to die. I am not going to die alone," the man's voice reportedly exclaimed.

Mrs. Dutchaellier's screams finally attracted enough attention for a neighbor to call the police. When they arrived, the police found that Mrs. Dutchaellier had been stabbed twice in the abdomen with a kitchen knife by Morreiset. When question, Morreiset said that the older woman had placed a voodoo curse on him and that she would not remove it. He told of the extreme bad luck he had been having since he had become aware of the spell she had cast upon him.

Curses, spells, and hexes are the evils of black magic, and just as evil are the spells inflicted on people "for their own good"—for how do we in truth know what is best for another? One system of spell-casting is called "rootwork." Aspects of many contemporary hex reports suggest the hand of a rootworker, and it is interesting to note here how and why a rootworker achieves his diabolical effects.

The phenomenon of rootwork was first explained by Dr. Ronald Wintrob, a Connecticut psychiatrist, in a recent article in Volume I of *Medical Opinion,* a scientific periodical. I am indebted to him for most of the following information on the subject.

Rootwork is an eclectic form of spell-casting derived from three sources: African witchcraft, Haitian voodoo, and European witchcraft. A rootworker casts a spell for another person and is also known as a rootdoctor, conjurer, or hoodoo man. He is believed to have great power in casting spells. The person hexed by a rootworker is said to be rooted, mojoed, hoodooed, or conjured.

Dr. Wintrob explains:

> *. . . rootwork is a highly organized system of beliefs shared by blacks who were raised in the Southeastern United States or who retain close ties there with family or friends. But, most importantly, rootwork is now reported as being practiced in cities across the nation, from Los Angeles to Tucson, New York and Detroit. And, it is no longer confined to the black community.*

The impetus for rootwork is most commonly rivalry or another kind of resentment. A love triangle is a common reason for much rootwork. The conjurer casts his spell by slipping powdered roots, powdered snake or frog, part of the victim's hair, nail parings, or excreta into his food or drink; or by simply placing the vile concoction near his doorstep or somewhere else around his residence. The effect of the spell on its victim is clinically describable: "The two most common disorders attributed to rootwork are psychiatric and extreme gastrointestinal conditions. One motif that crops up repeatedly involves the sensation of reptiles crawling over the skin."

Dr. Wintrob blames the flourishing of rootwork today on socioeconomic and political factors—the exclusion of blacks from the dominantly white community has brought about a sense of powerlessness, futility, and suppressed rage on the part of the blacks. "The greater the uncertainty of people about their chances of achieving socially valued goals, the greater the tendency to seek and accept alternative paths to these goals, magic among them."

And he sees no reason why a victim cannot be successfully treated by a medical doctor. But doctors must be flexible in dealing with a patient's beliefs, Wintrob emphasizes in his report. "To fail to take into account the patient's convictions about the cause of his condition makes it far more difficult to take an accurate history, conduct a medical exam or come up with a meaningful diagnosis." The attending physician should remember a most important dictum:

> *The patient's belief in rootwork or spells does not rule out treatment by health professionals. Nor does treatment by health professionals rule out treatment by rootworkers [rootworkers are also sought out by those who believe they have been cursed and who desire the spell neutralized, removed, or sent back to its original source]. Both therapies can be practiced in peaceful coexistence.*

Dr. Wintrob presents the following case study, based on records at Baltimore City Hospital in 1967, as an example of what can happen when a hex is placed on someone. A midwife had informed the mothers of three baby girls who had all been born near the Florida swamps that spells had been placed upon their daughters and that each of them would die young. The first child would die before her sixteenth birthday, the second before her twenty-first, and the third before her twenty-third birthday.

Several years passed, and the young girls grew up. The hospital first heard about the hex when the third woman was rushed there, apparently the victim of congestive heart failure. She was in a state of panic and was hyperventilating. Several days later, the story of the hexes was related to the hospital staff. The first girl had indeed died before her sixteenth birthday in an auto accident. The second had been at a nightclub actually celebrating the end of the hex on the eve of her twenty-first birthday when a fight broke out and several shots were fired. One bullet ricocheted off a table and killed her instantly.

The third girl did die in Baltimore City Hospital, of congestive heart failure.

Dr. Wintrob concludes:

> *This young lady's demise raises the question: Was she literally scared to death? Like a self-fulfilling prophecy, was her unshakable belief in her imminent death actually responsible for it, or was her fear only a contributory factor? Even if the heart disease was organic and ultimately fatal, her intense anxiety could have been alleviated by sensitive discussion with a physician, or by a visit from a rootdoctor.*

The current interest in the black arts is worldwide. In the early 'seventies the Reuters news agency reported that a heated debate had taken place in the House of Commons about the rise of witchcraft in England after the then home secretary, Henry Brooke, had told the House that it was not a crime to be a witch and that witchcraft had ceased to be a criminal offense in 1735. The debate had broken out when certain members had expressed concern about the ever-increasing number of offenses brought to public attention that involved witchcraft, black magic, and the like.

"It is not in my mind," said Lord Brooke, "two hundred and twenty-eight years later to bring in fresh legislation on the subject."

Recently, the Communist Youth newspaper *Komsomolskaya Pravada* reported that Agafya Kuchnova, a milkmaid in a village 150 miles from Moscow, had been branded as a witch by not only her neighbors but the local authorities as well.

It was Reuters who broke the story in the 'sixties of two elderly women who were found guilty of a witchcraft killing in the city of Salisbury, Rhodesia. The women were sentenced to death by the high courts. The prosecution said that the two had murdered one of the women's two-year-old grandson in a form of ritual in order to promote the sale of their home-brewed beers and liquors.

In the past several years, as I have noted, every major American monthly and weekly magazine has printed articles on the rise of interest in the occult, articles that have ranged from factual reports of what is happening to outright condemnations of black-magic practices. Most of the authors of these articles have agreed on one point, however, which concerns why this interest in the occult has occurred at this particular point in our history.

Bruce Cook, in the November, 1969, issue of *Catholic World,* summed up for the reasoning behind this truly amazing phenomenon when he said, "In any society which offers too much or too little chance for individual expression, there are bound to be alienated, disaffected individuals, those who feel themselves outside and absolutely opposed to the social order. Among these you will find the cultural have-nots, the criminal types, the psychopaths and psychotics, who today crowd our jails and mental institutions."

Another writer, Edward Gross, has suggested that interest in chance, magic, and the like is not so surprising when one looks around at our modern times. The unexplained and the terrifying were never so great as they are right now, this very minute. Scientifically, intellectually, we know more and more, but our sense of control hardly seems to grow at all, and nowhere is this more obvious than in our modern, congested cities.

Centuries ago, nature was the problem. One used to worry about being struck by lightning; now one worries about being burned in an electrical fire or an airplane crash. Wild animals and the fear they engendered has been replaced by another dread—a mugger or a gunman gone berserk. And worse are the evils we only dimly imagine—the hijacking Arab, the inscrutable Chinese, the military, the industrial complex, Wall Street, and others.

To the powerless, which so many of us seem to be today, *luck* has a most special appeal. For the unsuccessful, and particularly for those among them who find little reward for their merit and their efforts in personal spheres, the doctrines of *luck* (inherent in all forms of magic and the occult) serve the psychological function of enabling them to preserve their self-esteem in the face of failure. In this connection, witchcraft, the psychic sciences, Tarot cards, astrology have all been called socially legitimized randomizing devices.

Even the current "Jesus movement" has been blamed for sparking the rise in the worship of the devil and witchcraft. Many insist that Satan is necessary as a foil to Jesus—people who never even thought of the Devil before becoming involved in the Jesus movement. It is ironic that the movement may eventually do more to popularize Satan among the young than all the devil-freak cults put together.

In the late 'sixties, interest in the occult was supposed to be on the wane. Trend-watchers predicted that investigation into the supernatural was a passing fad. Publishers predicted that books on the subject would never sell.

But they were wrong. By the middle of 1973 news articles in *Time*, *Newsweek*, and elsewhere expressed more surprise than ever at the vast numbers of American citizens who were involving themselves in subjects beyond their usual realm of experience. Even the winding down of the Vietnam war—which might logically have enabled students who had tuned out of harsh reality to rejoin a better reality—seemed inexplicably to encourage interest in the supernatural.

There is a greater choice now of occult subjects taught and practiced in schools of higher learning than ever before. At Antioch College in Yellow Springs, Ohio, a five-credit course in astrology is offered. The University of Washington in Seattle lists courses in extrasensory perception, numerology, hypnotism, and yoga, all bearing academic credit. More than five hundred students signed up for a course in 1973 at the University of Wisconsin on astrology and witchcraft. At Boston College there is a three-credit course entitled "The Rhetoric of Dusk," taught by the speech-and-communications department, that consists of Monday-night lectures on devil worship, Satanism, witchcraft, and other occult subjects. At California State University in San Francisco, Dr. Charles Hagar, head of the astronomy department, uses astrology in his courses. Ethnopsychiatry (the study of how to heal mental disorders through supernatural powers such as witchcraft) is a subject offered to students by Philip Singer at Oakland University in California.

"The World of the Supernatural" is the name of a course taught at Pepperdine College in Los Angeles. Pepperdine is a usually ultraconservative school administered by the Church of Christ, but a sociology professor there, Laurence Keene, told the press he felt that if Pepperdine was a truly religious school, it should not be afraid of a legitimate study of the occult.

Florissant Valley College in St. Louis has lecture courses and workshops in the field of psychical studies. Its course on the occult, open to the public, was the most-attended noncredit course in the school's history.

Professor Iden Goodman, who teaches a popular seminar on dreams at California State University in San Francisco, gives probably the main reason for the ever-growing upsurgence of occult studies: "This huge desire for occult subjects is a reaction to our grossly materialistic culture. It is a part of the counter-culture's reaction against the rationalist, scientific tradition of Post-Renaissance Western thought." Many other educators agree and note that, in the past, periods of social upheaval have produced a vastly increased interest in the supernatural. I can't help but think that unless this current interest in the supernatural concentrates on its positive aspects, then the social upheaval now being felt will have horrible consequences.

CHAPTER 11

I didn't think about evil or the Devil until I was in my early twenties. My friend and teacher, Mae Aitken, who is mentioned earlier in this book, brought me to this awareness. Mrs. Aitken, a devout Spiritualist, turned to me during a conversation one day and said, "The Devil is walking on earth at the present time." What an odd thing to say, I recall thinking. We discussed her comment at length, and I found that Mrs. Aitken firmly believed, as did the other members of her congregation, that the Devil had managed to materialize in various physical forms and was commencing to wreak havoc and destruction on the earth in order to acquire the souls on it. As a recently lapsed Catholic, I was most skeptical of Mrs. Aitken's comments. One of the many reasons I had left the Church was because I had chosen not to believe in the Devil, or for that matter in such a place as hell.

I had this discussion with Mrs. Aitken in the early

'sixties. As that decade progressed, I began to realize that she indeed was correct—that the Devil, a negative energy, was on earth and was causing the horrendous effects that were so much a part of that era. The struggle between the powers of Darkness and Light hit an apex in the decade of the nineteen-sixties. Battles were won on both sides, but for the most part, it was evil which racked up a victory in that Dark era of spiritual evolvement.

Since the early twentieth century, scientists, philosophers, and others who live by the intellect have been saying that evil does not exist, that man has been steeped in superstition far too long, and that we should put aside childish, ungrounded fears. This is the twentieth century, they scream. It is time to cast off ideologies that concern the Devil, for there is no such thing.

So we relaxed our guard against the forces that we were beginning to feel were merely unintelligent superstitions of the past. We put our faith in science as the answer to everything.

By the nineteen-sixties we were at the point in our spiritual progress—or rather decline—at which we were able to say that God was no longer a reality. The "God is dead" movement reached its height in that decade, not only on the college campuses, but everywhere else in our society.

I do feel that the original purpose of those persons who first announced that "God is dead" was for people to recognize the fact that we might have been misinterpreting God in the past, that there should be a major reevaluation of God's place in this ever-changing society. But, as so often happens in learning, their words were taken literally. Millions of children and adults took to the belief that God indeed did not exist. (Curiously, there was no "the Devil is dead" movement.)

What followed after the "God is dead" movement were breakdowns on all levels of progress. The "I don't want to get involved" syndrome was born in the 'sixties. It is impossible even to imagine the vast numbers of persons who incurred karmic damage on their souls by standing by and allowing their fellowman to be harmed physically, mentally, or spiritually. Many people merely observed as those around cried out for assistance.

Assassinations were prevalent in the United States during the nineteen-sixties—the two Kennedys, Martin Luther King, and others. As I stated earlier, I believe that the assassins were tools of the evil that surfaced in this bleak era. It is not a coincidence that those persons who in some way spoke out for the Light, who had at least good intentions toward their fellowman, were ruthlessly murdered. Their annihilation seemed to emit an energy that held back from political progress those who had positive ideals and vibrations. Just look at who is in government office today on both local and national levels. The assassinations stopped when the positive political men were done away with.

The drug culture seemed to spring up overnight in the 'sixties. In its wake, hundreds of thousands of lives have been destroyed and their soul evolvement cut short by minds that were damaged or destroyed beyond repair.

The wasteful, pride-seeking efforts of man reached new heights of insanity in that decade: the senseless ego trips to the moon, costing billions of dollars, while on earth, in our own country, millions went hungry, lived in the vilest ghettos, went without a moment's education, and died from heart disease, cancer, or defective automobiles—all causes which might have been easily eradicated by using only a part of the money spent on those few rocks brought back to earth.

The 'sixties also saw climactic riots of all kinds—on

campuses, in the ghettos, on the streets. Whenever we picked up the newspapers, we read of another riot, if not in our own country, somewhere else. They were like a disease that spread. Any kind of peaceful negotiations were laughed at—or worse, leaders of such peace movements were killed.

The greatest victory of evil over Light was, of course, the Vietnam war. The entire decade was blighted by this ludicrous war. To this day, few persons know why the war was fought, or what was gained by it. It was hideousness regulated and prolonged by those on both sides who wished to use it for political or financial gain. It all but destroyed the fiber of American life, forcing people to take sides either for or against it, as if it were an elaborate game.

In "defending" South Vietnam, we destroyed it. Hundreds of thousands of Americans and Vietnamese were cut short of their karmic destiny, prevented from growing and reaching fruition because of the selfishness of the leaders of the countries involved. Some say that the souls who were involved in the war were meant to be, that the war was their karma. I believe that the war was new karma, that as with so many other situations in our time, we were presented with a choice, and that we chose to destroy rather than to attempt a peaceful means of settling the problem. The Vietnam war has horribly sullied the national karma of the United States, and we might not survive it as a nation.

The polarization of Americans hardened in the nineteen-sixties. Black against white. Hippie against hardhat. Youth against age. Right against left. The decade brought their differences out into the open, whereupon they exploded in mass violence and hatred instead of being solved in more positive ways. There were indeed good reasons for their coming to the fore, but the way they did so only added to the destructiveness inherent in the problems. I realize that this may sound idealistic, but I truly believe that we could have approached and confronted the forces that held the nineteen-sixties in their grip in more spiritual, positive ways. And we failed. We joined with and utilized the energy of the Darker forces, rather than recognizing the fact that it was evil that needed to be conquered, not the situations themselves.

Evidence of the Devil was continually prominent throughout the sixties. There seemed to me to be a flagrant downgrading of all things deemed "good" or positive—they were fashionably called silly or old-fashioned. I recall that many people I knew would ridicule and mock the likes of performers like Julie Andrews. I would tell them that I didn't understand, that I felt Julie Andrews was a consummate singer, a fine actress, a beautiful woman, and that she expressed qualities that were most positive. "She's too good," they would answer. "No one is *that* good. She's so *good* that it makes me sick!" Isn't it interesting that someone's goodness, when visible, can make others ill?

On the other hand, the more negative attributes our public figures displayed, the more they were sought after and placed on pedestals.

"The Devil is walking on the earth," Mrs. Aitken told me, and I now completely believe her. I have recently had arguments with certain students in my psychic-awareness classes who tell me that God and the Devil are one force, that good and evil stem from the same place, they are the same power, and it is the individual who chooses how he will use this power.

I firmly believe that good and evil are two completely different energies. It is the same in physics: protons have a positive charge and electrons a negative charge. They never are the same. Ruth Nanda Anshen, an editor of many humanistic periodicals and publications, says in her book *The Reality of the Devil*: "God's ways and the Devil's way part. There certainly is greatness on each side. We may with certainty rely on God or the Devil. The choice is ours."

How can we not recognize a force that has not only been identified but named throughout the centuries? The ancient Iranians called this force Manyu, "prince of Darkness." In Siberia the Devil is referred to as the Great Crow, or Ngaa. American Indian tribes refer to the Devil as Coyote or Gluskap. Slavic peoples refer to the Devil as Dis.

Earlier I spoke of Satan and Lucifer. Throughout history, in every civilization, in almost every religion, the force that is evil has been named and spoken of as having a true, physical body, or at least physical forms which can be manifested. The universality of this belief in the corporality of the Devil makes one stop and think about the many people who have been put in institutions after claiming that they have seen the Devil, conversed with him, or made a pact with him.

A current comedian's famous line is "The Devil made me do it!" Everyone laughs, but beneath the laughter there is more than a tinge of uneasiness. We have all done things that we could have sworn sprang from somewhere other than our own being or subconscious. I believe that one reason the highest percentage of suicides in any profession happens among psychiatrists is that they are unable to cope with the unbelievable number of stories they must hear from patients who have been utilized by an evil force.

Scientists now agree that there are forces in our universe that are dangerous and unhealthy. They have not yet decided whether the forces are natural or supernatural. They openly admit that those persons throughout history who created what is called a "mythology of the Devil" were doing it mainly for protection from evil, whether based in fact or fantasy.

Our scientifically oriented universe of the past hundred years, ripe with fruits of technology, was expected to eliminate any hypothesis claiming the existence of the Devil, as a person or as a force. Psychology and politics were looked to as the cure for evildoing perpetrated by countries, groups, and individuals. The battle that our forefathers fought throughout the centuries against evil, waged in the churches and in their own minds, afforded them protection against it. We have thrown off this protection by intellectually denying the existence of evil.

As Dr. Andrew M. Greeley, head of the Study of American Pluralism of the National Opinion Research Center, University of Chicago, and the man whose article I quoted extensively in the previous chapter, recently said in *The New York Times:*

> *If there is a superintelligence guiding the powers of evil, one must say that his strategy has been brilliant; the situation in Europe in the early nineteen-forties, while Russia and Germany were simultaneously governed by madmen, was a stroke of incomparable evil genius. If all the disasters that afflicted the United States in the ninteen-sixties were the result of random choice, then we were extraordinarily unlucky. If one believes in personified evil, then one must say that the nineteen-sixties were one of his finest hours.*

In my autobiography, *The Reluctant Prophet*, I made a prediction concerning the Catholic Church. As far back as the late nineteen-fifties I had said that I felt the Church would completely modernize itself and eventually become, in this century, a powerful, modern force; that it would make momentous changes in itself and become a leader, by the end of the century, which would utilize the power of Light, after having spent hundreds of years in the Dark. I still believe this to be true. In 1972, a speech delivered by Pope Paul VI was condemned by many progressive Catholics both in the Church and out because of its contents, which I find to be of most importance to those who are beginning to realize that the forces of evil are indeed manifest in many forms. Paul VI said:

> *What are the greatest needs of the Church today? Do not let our answer surprise you as being over-simple or even superstitious and unreal: One of the greatest needs is defense from the evil which is called the Devil. . . .*
>
> *Do we not see how much evil there is in the world today? Particularly, how much moral evil, simultaneously, though in different ways, against man and against God? Is this not a sorry spectacle, an inexplicable mystery? Is it not we followers of the Word, we believers, who are most sensitive, most upset by the observation and experience of evil?*
>
> *We find sin the perversion of human freedom, and the deep cause of death, because it is separation from God, good, the source of life, and then in its turn, the occasion and effect of an intervention in us and in our world of an obscure agent, the Devil. Evil is not merely a lack of something, but an effective agent, a living spiritual being, perverted and perverting. A terrible reality. Mysterious and frightening.*
>
> *It is contrary to the teaching of the Bible and the Church to refuse to recognize the existence of such a reality, or to regard it as a principle in itself which does not draw its origin from God like every other creature; or to explain it as a pseudoreality, a conceptual and fanciful personification of the unknown causes of our misfortunes. The problem of evil, seen in its complexity, and its absurdity from the viewpoint of our one-sided rationality, becomes an obsession. It is the greatest difficulty for our religious understanding of the cosmos. . . .*

That it is not a question of one Devil, but of many, is indicated by various passages in the Gospel. But the principal one is Satan, which means the adversary, the enemy: and with him many, all creatures of God, but fallen, because of their rebellion and damnation, a whole mysterious world, upset by an unhappy drama, of which we know very little.

So we know that this dark and disturbing Spirit really exists, and that he still acts with treacherous cunning; he is the secret enemy that sows errors and misfortunes in human history. He is the treacherous and cunning enchanter, who finds his way into us by way of the senses, the imagination, utopian logic and disorderly social contacts in the give and take of life, to introduce deviations, as harmful as they are apparently in conformity with our physical or psychical structures, or our deep, instinctive aspirations.

This question of the Devil and the influence he can exert on individual persons as well as on communities, whole societies or events, is a very important chapter of Catholic doctrine which is given little attention today, though it should be studied again. Some people think a sufficient compensation can be found in psychoanalytical and psychiatric studies or in spiritualistic experiences, so widespread, unfortunately, in some countries today. People are afraid of falling into old Manichean theories again, or into frightening divagations of fancy and superstition. Today people prefer to appear strong and unprejudiced, to pose as positivists, while at the same time giving credit to so many unwarranted magical or popular superstitions. Worse, they are opening their souls to the licentious experiences of the senses, and to the harmful ones of drugs, as well as to the ideological seductions of fashionable errors, cracks through which the Devil can easily penetrate and work upon the human mind.

Many of the new Catholics were literally embarrassed by this speech, calling it one more lamentable Pauline *faux pas.* Years ago, before I had experienced firsthand many of the evils the Pope spoke of, I would have been first in line to speak out against such a speech. Today I can only hope that his words will help to halt the ever-increasing tide of the evil forces.

EPILOGUE

I HAVE HAD MORE OF WHAT ONE MIGHT TERM "BAD LUCK" since the commencement of writing this book than I have ever had before in my entire life. In earlier chapters, I have related occurrences that were almost overpowering as I was in the midst of the manuscript.

The forces of evil, which I firmly believe have tried to prevent my completing this book, attacked almost every day that I worked on it. There was an endless battle, and had I not been aware, had I not sought self-protection, I would most certainly have given up.

Exactly one year from the very week of my first car accident, I was involved in another car crash. This one happened about two miles from the scene of the previous accident under the same weather conditions. My new car was struck on the same side, resulting in exactly the same amount of damage. I was once again, most fortunately, not injured.

During the year that I took to write this book, I developed a major illness which could not be diagnosed for months. After a weight loss of forty pounds, I was told that the disease (a stomach disorder) occurs in one out of ten thousand persons.

Major personal changes took place in this time, most of them quite unpleasant. I lost several very close friends. Financial difficulties were an ever-increasing problem. Everything, in fact, that might prevent my getting to the typewriter in a proper frame of mind occurred in this period.

An incredible thing happened to me at the New York Public Library. I had requested that any information on witchcraft and black magic be lent to me so that I could run it through the microfilm viewer and complete my research. As I was copying down some of the material, the machine suddenly began to smoke—and the film disintegrated before my eyes! If that wasn't reason enough to run and take cover during research on the black arts, nothing would be!

Even devoted friends and editors told me that the book wasn't worth the clear-cut risks I was taking. But I was determined to finish the manuscript. The attacks only made me realize how important it was for me to publish the work.

Even getting the completed parts of the book to the publisher became almost impossible. On the last two days that I was finishing up rewrites, I developed an ear infection. It became worse, and I went to a specialist. He diagnosed the problem as an abscess and proceeded to give me penicillin, having noted that I was not allergic to the drug. However, unbeknown to either of us, I had developed an allergy to penicillin. I immediately developed a very serious reaction to the drug and was rushed to the hospital. I was given antiallergy medication. The ear infection continued for weeks.

As soon as I did finish the book and give it to my publisher, my "luck" began to change. Business and personal problems cleared up, and my health improved tremendously. It was with a sigh of relief that I wrote the last words of this narrative. This may perhaps sound overdramatic, but I really did not think that I was going to make it. In fact, as I was being taken to the hospital, I bade farewell to my friends in the car. I was convinced that I was going to die.

I do believe that if it were not for the protection I had learned to afford myself, I would not be here today. The Darker forces would have won their victory. But perhaps my year of trial will serve as a warning for those who underestimate the pwer of evil, and as an inspiration to those who underestimate the power of good.

BIBLIOGRAPHY

Boudon, David, "An Eccentric Body of Art," *Saturday Review* (February, 1973), pp. 30–32.

Edwards, Henry, "Out of School with Alice Cooper," *After Dark* (October, 1972), pp. 18–23.

Eisle, James, *Psychic* (November-December, 1972), p. 32.

Goodwin, John, *Occult America* (New York: Doubleday, 1972).

Greeley, Andrew, "The Devil, You Say," *The New York Times Magazine* (February 4, 1973), p. 15.

Hansen, Chadwick, *Witches of Salem* (New York: George Braziller, 1969).

Merla, Patrick, "What is REAL Asked the Rabbit One Day," *Saturday Review* (November, 1972), pp. 42–50.

Robbins, Russell H., *The Encyclopedia of Witchcraft and Demonology* (New York: Crown Publishers, 1967).

Sanders, Ed, *The Family* (New York: Dutton, 1971).

———, "Charlie and the Devil," *Esquire* (November, 1972), p. 105.

Wheatley, Dennis, *The Devil and All His Works* (New York: American Heritage Press, 1972).

INDEX

Logan, Daniel, 1936-
America bewitched